Hell's Bells

Paperback Version

This book is a work of non-fiction. Unless otherwise noted, the author and the publisher make no explicit guarantees as to the accuracy of the information contained in this book.

© 2012 Ernest Johnson. All rights reserved.

No part of this book may be reproduced, stored in a retrieval system, or transmitted by any means without the written permission of the author.

First published 2012
Electronically published 2012 by Karah Kious-McJoslin, KarahbarkDesigns.com

ISBN: 978-0-9882803-1-1

Hell's Bells 1
THE BEAST IDENTIFIED...3
   THE BEAST IDENTIFIED...7
   THE BEAST DESCRIBED..22
   THE SATANIC CHURCH 27
   THE MARK OF THE BEAST 40
   THE IMAGE OF THE BEAST..46
   THE GLOBAL CONFLICT...54
   BABYLON THE GREAT THE MOTHER OF ALL 60
   WHO ARE YOU GOING TO LISTEN TO?........................62
REVELATION Q&A 66
THE GOD OF THIS WORLD 106
   SPIRIT AND SOUL 108
   SPIRITUAL BEINGS AND EARTHLY EVOLUTION 110
   AHRIMAN IN MODERN TIMES....................................114
   THE DEGRADATION OF LANGUAGE 115
   THE AHRIMANIZATION OF CULTURE.......................117
   GOOD AND EVIL 119
   THE CHRIST 120
      LUCIFER & AHRIMAN 120
      WHEN AND WHERE 121
      SOME OCCULT HISTORY.......................................122
   BRUTAL AND SPIRITUAL SCIENCE 125
   666 AGAIN 126
   TRUE AND FALSE 128
   THE TRUE SECOND COMING.....................................129
   OCCULT MEANING OF THE COMPUTER...................132
   AN EVOLUTIONARY LEAP 133
   TURNING EVIL TO GOOD 135
   THE EPOCH OF CONSCIOUSNESS..............................135
   SOME OCCULT POLITICS..138
THE ENOCHIAN APOCALYPSES..................................141
   A SAINT AND A ROGUE 141
   THE REALITY OF THE ENOCHIAN ANGELS 143
   THE GATES AND KEYS 143

THE NATURE OF THE APOCALYPSE 145
ENTER THE GREAT BEAST 148
A MENTAL ARMAGEDDON 150
About the Author 153

THE BEAST IDENTIFIED

Based on National Sunday Law A. Jan Marcussen

The nation trembles, passenger jets explode into buildings. Mountains of steel, smoke; and terrified people, fall to the street together as sky-scrapers crumble in the dust. Thousands perish. America is at war. A new kind of war fills our minds with pictures of strange faces, balls of fire, women screaming. Dust-filled people-like mummies-running from the cloud jam the bridges. "Were at war," the President said. The world will never be the same. Will terrorism, like some giant octopus engulf the world? Or will World War Three end at all!

We're going to go now on an incredible journey behind the scenes and take a shocking glimpse. Something's happening in our country, something strange. Have you noticed the trends? Thirty-eight people looking out their windows in a New York City, watched a murder that took a full half an hour to commit, and did nothing about it! Thirty-eight people watched Catherine Genovese being stabbed again and again in front of her home, and didn't care. They just leaned out their windows as if watching the late show, waited "till it was over, and went back to bed!"

Since America was attacked, are things different now? Get ready for a shock. You're going to go behind the scenes, and see awesome things that are happening- leading to a great crisis in our land. It all starts on a stark, rocky island. Into the horizon stretches that vast expanse of the murky deep. One lone figure rests on a barren ledge of sheer rock. His name is John the Revelator. What he sees is fantastic! Strange beasts, clashing armies and nations rising and falling. It's no surprise that the greatest nation on earth should be mentioned in prophecy. What John sees portends events shaping up in the United States that most definitely will affect you. Watch closely now as the scene unfolds.

Rev.13:11- {"And I saw another beast coming up out of the earth; and he had two horns like a lamb, and he spoke as a dragon."}

A "beast" in prophecy represents a "kingdom." Read Daniel 7:23. When a beast comes out of the "sea," it is represented in prophecy as rising amid many "peoples and multitudes," A highly populated area. Read Rev.17:15. To come up out of the "earth" is just the opposite. So here we have a nation that is springing up out of a wilderness area. Instead of overthrowing vast and well trained armies from dense populations of the world, this nation would be an area "discovered." In the eyes of the "known world," it would be new territory. Differing from the often blood-soaked nations of Europe, it would spring up quietly, peacefully, "like a lamb."

Can you guess what nation of the "new world" arose into power, giving promises of strength and greatness that would fit this description? Sure! The United States of America. It sprang up like a plant from the ground. A prominent author from a hundred years age; speaks of "the mystery of her coming forth from vacancy," and adds; "like a silent seed we grew into an empire." The pilgrims and settlers met up with Indian tribes, but compared to the crowded cities and millions of the old world, America was a wilderness. "And he had two horns like a lamb" The lamb-like horns indicate youth, gentleness, and represent civil and religious freedom. The declaration of Independence and the Constitution reflect these noble views. Because of these very principles, our nation became great. The oppressed and persecuted from all lands looked to the U.S. with hope. But the beast with the lamb-like horns spoke as a dragon.

Rev.13:11-13-{And I saw another beast coming up out of the earth; and he had two horns like a lamb and he spoke as a dragon. And he exercises all the authority of the first beast in his presence. And he makes the earth and those who dwell in it to worship the first beast whose fatal wound was healed. And he performs great signs, so that he even makes fire come down out of heaven to the earth in the presence of men.}

Incredible! Keep your eyes open. As the drama unfolds, you will see miracles of the most amazing nature! Rev.13:14-{And he deceives those who dwell on the earth because of the signs which it was given him to perform in the presence of the beast, telling those who dwell on the earth to make an image to the beast who had the wound of the sword and has come to life.}

Can you imagine the United States doing any thing this incredible? Not me! I don't think the United States is that smart. How could this possible happen? Watch closely! The lamb-like horns and then the dragon voice present a change of personality. A real change! The speaking of this country as a "dragon" denotes the use of force. This principle, as we shall see, was used by the leopard-like beast (the first beast) of Rev.13, which enforced religious observances by law!

Such action by the U.S. Constitution provides that "Congress shall make no law respecting an establishment of religion, of prohibiting the free exercise thereof." "Speak as a dragon"-our nation? Do you hear it stirring?

Have you noticed attitudes becoming more intolerant and angry lately-angry at crime; terrorism; political, religious, and social corruption? In view of the horrifying trends of the time, it's understandable why the nation is to "speak" that way. In one year, Americans spent 4 billion on pornography. Mass murders, neglect of the aged, abuse of women and even babies, sickens the heart. Men possessed are taking the lives of men, women, and children. Millions of Americans, hooked on methamphetamine, "crack," heroin, and other chemicals, peer at the world through differing degrees of "goony eyes," and further appall society with their resultant behavior and crimes. A recent report to the Federal Communications Commission states, "between the ages of 5 and 14 the average American child witnesses the violent destruction of thirteen thousand human beings on television."

A U.S. senate subcommittee revealed that in one decade violence witnessed on T.V. skyrocketed and delinquency in real life grew nearly 200%! Movies and internet garbage too horrible to mention fill the minds of young and old. Prostitutes, homosexuals, and drug addicts share AIDS with the innocent. The poor suffers give groans of despair as they perish in ever greater numbers. A group of them, LIFE magazine reported, lying on the floor in a circle, and summoning some of their remaining strength-laughed in sequence. In the words of one commentator, "Surely America stumbles headlong toward the final precipice. Tripped on the downward road of immorality, it plunges with ever-increasing momentum toward the point of no return. Crime doubles every ten years. Political and religious corruption has caused even the Constitution to come under attack!

People are angry. The nation is angry. The shifting of values and anger of the times (in speedy fulfillment of prophecy) are echoed in words blurted out by a Jesuit Priest-"I just don't understand the reverence which everybody here seems to pay to the American Constitution. I want to hear some American get up and shout, give us justice. Give us decency. And to hell with the American Constitution."

Is it any wonder that our nation will "speak as a dragon?" Little wonder that ministers across the land, in an effort to abort national doom, move millions to political action. The feeling is that something must be done. Leaders of the "electronic church" launched a campaign to arouse 50 million Christians! There's a tremendous drive on to unite forces for the common good.

Pat Robertson said, "Unless Christians desire a nation and a world reordered to the humanistic model; it is absolutely vital that we take control of the U.S. government away from the trilateral Commission and the Council on Foreign Relations." He speaks of turning to God "to galvanize Christians to political action." U.S. NEWS & WORLD REPORT declared, "A political holy war without precedent is in full swing in this country."

The feeling is being spread that only if our nation comes back to God can we improve our sorry state of affairs. Leaders are saying that this can be accomplished if Christians unite. Robert Grant, leader of "Christian Voice" urged: "If Christians unite, we can do anything. We can pass any law or any amendment. And that's exactly what we intend to do." On nation-wide T.V. he declared: "We can do anything, we can amend the Constitution. We can elect a president. We can change or make any law in the land. And it behooves us to do it. If we have to live under law, as well we should, we should live under moral and Godly law."

This is not the opinion of just one man. In a letter to the leader of the "Religious Roundtable" he asked if it is time for someone to influence legislation to make Sunday a day of worship in our country. In reply, the executive director, H. Edward Rowe wrote, "Legislation and proclamations by Presidents to urge it, Yes!"

The dynamics make us wonder little that nation-wide papers and media messages have pled to the masses that it is the responsibility of government to decree the establishment of the national observance of Sunday, and that there will be no relief from mounting economic disaster until a national Sunday law is strictly enforced! It's not surprising that in a hearing of the South Carolina legislature, demands by State Representative Anderson himself for a Sunday law to improve the state of society brought uproarious applause. Who can wonder that the United States president has revealed his willingness to support legislation which would help collapse the separation of church and state!

"And he spoke as a dragon. And he exercises all power of the first beast before him." Rev.13:11.12. We have not seen anything yet! Be prepared to learn some shocking facts. Here is the big question now- who is this God damn beast?

THE BEAST IDENTIFIED

Rev.13:1-{And I stood on the sand of the seashore. And I saw a beast coming up out of the sea, having ten horns and seven heads, and on his horns were ten diadems, and on his heads were blasphemes names.}

Here is the God damned beast that has the dreaded mark. This mark we definitely do not want! The most awful warning of all time is directed against it. Rev.14:9.10 tells us that if we take this dreaded mark our soul is damned for all eternity. This is why I will call this the God damned mark of the beast because it is God damned all the way around.

Before we learn what the God damned mark is, we must discover who the God damned beast is. And it won't be God damned hard either. In fact, the Bible makes it so God damned clear that I'll list the characteristics of it and you will be able to tell me who it is! Are you God damned ready! Here we go-

(1) A "beast" in prophesy represents a kingdom, a nation, a power. The prophetic book of Daniel tells us –"Thus he said, the fourth beast shall be the fourth kingdom upon the earth." Daniel 7:24.

(2) This beast comes out of the "sea." When a beast arises from the "sea," it represents a power rising in a highly populated area; amid "peoples, and multitudes, and nations, and tongues." Rev. 17:15. It would have to conquer the existing government.

(3) This God damn beast has seven heads and ten horns. A head represents the headquarters of a government. The head of a county is called the "county seat," you remember. A "horn represents a king, a ruler. "And the ten horns out of this kingdom are ten kings that shall arise." Daniel 7:24. The beast is a power with a man at the head of it. You will find that the Bible explains itself!

(4) The God damned beast has "the name of blasphemy." Rev.13:1. What is blasphemy? Again the Bible gives its own definition. In John 10:32.33, it tells how the Jews were going to stone Jesus. He asked them why they were about to stone Him and they said, "For a good reason we stone you not; but for blasphemy; and because that thou, being a man, make your self God."

Amazing! Blasphemy is for a man to claim to be God! Of course Jesus did not blaspheme because He is God. But for someone less than God- it would be. But there's God damn more.

In Mark 2:3-11, it tells the story of how a paralyzed man wanted to come into a house where Jesus was, but it was just too crowded. He finally persuaded his friends to carry him up on the roof of Peters' house and break it up so they could let the man down into the room where Jesus the Savior was teaching. So down he comes. Jesus looked into those pleading eyes and knows that the poor man needs to have forgiveness and peace with God even more than physical healing, Jesus says to him, "Son, thy sins be forgiven you." Mark 2:5

Can you imagine the wonderful peace and joy that flooded his soul? But the religious leaders did not care a thing about the man's soul. They were just trying to catch some words out of Jesus that they could use against Him to have Him put to death. The Bible says that they thought, "Why does this man thus speak blasphemes? Who can forgive sins but God only?"

The Savior knew their thoughts and said, "Why reason you these things in your hearts?" Then He asked them which is easier to say, "thy sins be forgiven," or to say, "arise" and walk?

Jesus healed the man before their eyes, and, to the people's utter amazement, he got up and walked out of the house. Again, Jesus did not commit blasphemy by forgiving the man's sins because He is a member of the Godhead and had a perfect right to do that. To whomever He pleased He could say those sweet words of forgiveness, and the very peace of heaven would flood the soul. He could say, "Go and sin no more," and the guilty, depressed, sad and empty, would rise up with peace of mind. They would begin a new and unselfish life of obedience to God and a happy life of peace and joy.

They could slap Him in the face and press a crown of thorns onto that holy brow; they could beat Him until His back was like raw meat, but they could not rob Him of His royal right to forgive the chief of sinners. Wonderful Jesus! But for anyone less than God to claim to forgive sins- it is blasphemy.

Concerning the beast, "And upon his head the name of blasphemy." Rev.13:1 The very leaders of this power would both claim to be God on the earth, and claim to have power to forgive men's sins!

  (5) And the dragon gave him his power, and his seat, and great authority." Rev.13:2. It is clear that the beast gets its "seat" and "authority" from the dragon. But who is the God damned dragon?

Here it is. Rev.20:2-{And he laid hold of the dragon, the serpent of old, who is the devil and Satan, and bound him for a thousand years.} The dragon is Satan. But there is more.

Rev.12:3-5-"{And there appeared another wonder in heaven; and behold a great dragon, having seven heads and ten horns, and seven crowns upon his heads. And his tail drew the third part of the stars of heaven, and did cast them to earth; and the dragon stood before the woman which was ready to be delivered, for to devour her child as soon as it was born. And she brought forth a man child, who was to rule all nations with a rod of iron: and her child was caught up unto God, and to his throne."}

Rev.19:15.16-shows us that Christ is the man child. So the "dragon" represents not only Satan, but also a kingdom through whom Satan worked to try to kill baby Jesus as soon as He was born. Now what kingdom was it whose king decreed the destruction of the babies in Bethlehem? Of course! It was King Herod. He was employed by, and a representative of Rome. So here's another clue. The God damned beast gets its power, seat, and authority from God damned Rome!

It is coming clear. The dragon represents God damned Rome. Rome was the God damned empire used by Satan to try to destroy the Savior of the world! Now let's take a closer look. The dragon (Rome) had "ten horns." A horn grows out of the head of an animal. A horn, you remember, is a king. When the Roman Empire collapsed, ten divisions resulted. Barbarian tribes hammered at the Roman Empire for many years until it fell apart and the ten divisions were ruled by ten kings! They were: the Alemani (Germany), the Franks (France), Burgundians (Switzerland), the Suevi (Portugal), The anglo Saxons (Britain), the Visigoths (Spain), The Lombards (Italy), the Vandals, Ostrogoths, and Heruli. The last three were destroyed by the pope because they refused to become "Christian." The armies of Emperor Justinian, in cooperation with the pope, thrust the Ostrogoths out of the city of Rome. They have become extinct. In 538 A.D. the pope took possession of the city after the emperor decreed that he should be the head of all the Christian churches. These ten divisions of Rome are the ten horns on the "dragon." Now look at this-

(6) "And all that dwell on the earth shall worship him, whose name are not written in the book of life of the lamb slain from the foundation of the world." Rev.13:8. This is not only a political power but a religious power as well. It demands worship and gets it.

(7) Rev.13:13- {And he performs great signs, so that he even makes fire come down out of heaven to the earth in the presence of men.} This is a world wide power. This is also a world of television and camcorders. "All the world did wonder after the beast." Many of you already know who the "beast" is. Let me ask you this. Is there any other world-wide political and religious power with a man at the head of it who claims to be God on this earth who has the power to forgive sins? Who received its seat from Rome? Of a church government whose leader is "wondered after" by the whole world?

Let me say something here that is very important. You see, the reason why God speaks as strongly against worshiping the "beast' as He does is because He loves the people. He loves all people. Dear reader, He loves you too. He knows that a person cannot possibly be happy who follows this blasphemous power and receives its mark. He knows that they will have no rest day or night.

Rev.14:11- {"And the smoke of their torment goes up forever and ever; and they have no rest day and night, those who worship the beast and his image, and whoever receives the mark of his name."}

It's clear from this Scripture that there is eternal damnation associated with it. If fact it is God damned guaranteed. God loves you so much that He has warned you in the strongest language possible. Listen to this-

Rev.14:9.10-{And another angel, a third one, following them, saying with a loud voice, "If anyone worships the beast and his image, and receives a mark on his forehead or upon his hand, he will also will drink of the wine of the wrath of God, which is mixed in full strength in the cup of His anger; and he will be tormented with fire and brimstone in the presence of the holy angels and in the presence of the Lamb."}

This is the strongest language that I know of. It sounds pretty crystal clear to me. Language of love is always strong when it is a question of life and death to the one it loves.

Let me ask you what more could God possible do for you. He sent His only begotten Son to die for you, yet you will go and serve this beast. God is a jealous God and He is jealous for your love. Jesus even went through hell for you, literally. He does not want anyone to experience this awful fate called damnation.

Jesus is your only way out friend. He suffered agony of Gethsemane and the torture of His mock trial where they beat His back until it was raw meat. They bowed down in mockery and hit Him in the head with a stick-driving the thorns into His brow and sending blood running down His sweet face. They watched Him stagger on His way to Calvary. The Son of God falls on His face down into the dirt along the way. He endured this horror. This is the horror of our sins. He did nothing but suffer all the way. Jesus went down. Jesus took the heat off of you and I. He lost lots of blood along the way. His blood ran drop by drop to the foot of the cross. Then with quivering lips he cries "My God, My God, why hast Thou forsaken Me?" Then you think you have the right to go out and serve a false god. This is why God is mad. There has been a lot of serving false gods in this old world and Jehovah is getting pretty darn tired of it. This is His way of putting an end to it on this earth.

There He hangs –like a snake on a pole, writhing in agony, drinking the last drop of the wrath of God against sin. "As Moses lifted up the serpent in the wilderness," Jesus was also lifted up-for you and I. Do you understand now what I am telling you? He did it for you. He took upon himself the horrors and the death from sin that you and I deserve; because in God's eyes you and I deserve to die. We deserve eternal punishment, but Jesus became our escape.

He took the rap for us. Can you understand now why our Heavenly father is so anxious that we not follow the beast or receive its mark? We need not receive that bad old penalty. Jesus paid your penalty in full for you and me. Receive it because if you don't then you will pay for it in eternity through eternity. You will be God damned forever.

Now get this, When they were pounding stakes through His flesh, what did He pray? He prayed "Father, forgive them for they do not know what it is they do." He bought you with His precious blood life giving blood. Receive it or be damned. Will you choose to follow the Christ and receive Him as your personal Lord and Savior from sin and death, and follow Him all the way?

You will be happy you did. Or hell fire brimstone if you don't. Choose now. Now is the time for salvation. Put away malice, strife and divisions. Put away all the dead works of the flesh. Realize your need for a Savior. Trusting Him; obeying Him; abiding in His love through prayer and Bible study; total surrender, and a loving, happy relationship- only then will you be safe from worshipping the beast and receiving his "mark"- only then.

Soon you will see why. In identifying the beast, God is not talking about sincere people who are involved with it "ignorantly." Do you know what I mean? When He identifies it, He is talking about "those deliberately disobey and change the word of God." Do you see? Our God is a tender Father. He only holds accountable those who understand what the Bible commands, and knowingly disobey, or those who turn away from hearing His word are "willingly ignorant."

The beast exists now. Many honest Christians who are now involved with it will soon learn the facts about it. They will hear God's call to come out of it. And they will respond. Many will not. Don't be fooled by thinking the "beast is a computer" in Europe somewhere. That is only a smoke screen to get people off track that the Bible points out. God's word makes it so clear that even an honest child can see it. The next point in identifying the beast is amazing.

(8) It has characteristics of the four beasts (nations) which existed before it. Watch closely-
Rev.13:2-{And the beast which I saw was like a leopard, and his feet were like those of a bear, and his mouth like the mouth of a lion. And the dragon gave him his power and his throne and great authority.} What nations are these? Again the Bible tells us. The same four beasts are in Daniel 7. "These great beasts, which are four, are four kings, which shall rise out of the earth." Daniel 7:17.

These are the four world empires, riling consecutively from the time of Daniel down to the time of the fall of Rome. They are Babylon {605-538 B.C.}, Medo-Persia {538_331 B.C.}, Greece {331-168B.C.}, and Rome {168 B.C.-476A.D.}. Now let's get the full description of these in Daniel 7.

"Daniel spoke and said, 'I saw my vision by night, and behold, the four winds of the heaven strove upon the great sea. And four beasts came up out of the sea, diverse one from another.'"

Daniel 7:2-8- {Daniel said, "I was looking in my vision by night, and behold, the four winds of heaven were stirring up the great sea. And the four beasts were coming up from the sea, different from one another. The first was like a lion, and had the wings of an eagle. I kept looking until its wings were plucked, and it was lifted up from the ground and made to stand on two feet like a man; a human mind (heart) was given it. And behold, another beast, a second one, resembling a bear. And it was raised up on one side, and three ribs were in its mouth between its teeth; and thus they said to it, 'Arise and devour much meat!' After this I kept looking, and behold, another one, like a leopard, which had on its back four wings of a bird; the beast also had four heads, and dominion was given to it. After this I kept looking in the night visions, and behold, a fourth beast, dreadful and terrifying and extremely strong; and it had large iron teeth. It devoured and crushed, and trampled sown the remainder with its feet; and it was different from all the beasts that were before it, and it had ten horns. While I was contemplating the horns, behold, another horn, a little one, came up among them, and three of the first horns were pulled out by the roots before it; and behold, this (in this horn were eyes) possessed eyes like the eyes of a man, and a mouth uttering great boasts."}

What a picture! Here they are, beginning with Daniels day- The Lion-Babylon, The Bear-Medo-Persia, The Leopard-Greece, The Terrible Beast-Rome.

Since the beast with the mark has similarities of these four, let's take a close look at them. Babylon (represented by the two winged lion) ruled the world when Daniel was alive. In the ruins of the ancient city of Babylon, broken statues of lions with two wings have been seen.

The Lion is a fit symbol of Babylon. It was the greatest of all ancient kingdoms. The two wings tell of swiftness in which the "golden kingdom" conquered the civilized world of that time. How is the "beast" of Rev. 13 like Babylon?

Ancient Babylon founded by Nimrod (see Genesis 10) the great grandson of Noah (more than two thousand years before Christ) was one of the wonders of the world. It was laid out in a perfect square with a great high wall eighty-seven feet thick. Its two hundred and twenty five square miles of enclosed surface was laid out in beautiful symmetry and interspersed with luxuriant pleasure grounds and gardens. With its sixty miles of moat, its sixty miles of outer wall. Its gates of solid brass, its hanging gardens, its subterranean tunnel under the River Euphrates, its perfect arrangement for beauty and defense-this city, containing in itself many things which were themselves wonders of the world, was itself another and still is a mightier wonder.

The emperors of Babylon claimed worship as gods. For man to be appreciated is great, but to be worshiped by other humans is blasphemes. The leader of the "beast" does this very thing! What about the next kingdom?

Medo-Persia took over on that terrible night when King Besshazzer, the last king of Babylon, half drunk, threw a party for a thousand of his lords and tossed the sacred vessels from the temple of God about the floor. That was the last straw. His knees knocked together in fear as he watched a bloodless hand trace his doom upon the palace wall. Look at this description of that fearful night.

Daniel 5:1.3.5-{Belshazzer the king held a great feast for a thousand of his nobles, and he was drinking wine in the presence of the thousand. Then they brought the gold vessels that had been taken out of the temple, the house of God which was in Jerusalem; and the king and his nobles, his wives, and his concubines drank from them. Suddenly the fingers of a man's hand emerged and began writing opposite the lamp stand on the plaster of the wall of the king's palace, and the king saw the back of the hand that did the writing.}

What a scene! At the sight of that bloodless hand, Belshazzer is paralyzed with fear. He calls in all the "astrologers, the Chaldeans, and the soothsayers," but they are no help. Finally, the queen suggests that Daniel be called in. The corrupt king is not ignorant of the fact that Daniel had shown himself able to interpret dreams and solve mysteries, because the God of heaven was with him. But Belshazzer hates God and doesn't even class Daniel with the wise men.

But now! Now he is scared to death. At the queen's suggestion Daniel is called in. Watch what happens-

Daniel 5:13- {Then Daniel was brought in before the king. The king spoke and said to Daniel, "Are you that Daniel who is one of the exiles from Judah, whom my father the king brought from Judah?"}

After mentioning the failure of his magicians to read the writing on the wall, the king said, Daniel 5:16-{"But I personally have heard of you, that you are able to give interpretations and solve difficult problems. Now if you are able to read the inscription and make its interpretation known to me, you will be clothed with purple and wear a necklace of gold around your neck, and you will have authority as the third ruler in the kingdom."}

Daniel well knew what would happen that night, and earthly rewards sank into nothingness. In a few hours, most in that court would be dead. He had no heart for rewards.

Daniel 5:17-{Then Daniel answered and said before the king. "Keep your gifts for yourself, or give your rewards to someone else; however, I will read the inscription to the king and make the interpretation known to him."}

After reminding the king of his rebellion and pride against God, he told him what the writing meant. Now comes the shocking news.

Daniel 5:25-28-{"Now this is the inscription that was written out: 'MENE, MENE, TEKAL, UPHARSIN.'" (A shekel from verb "to weigh") This is the interpretation of the message: 'MENE'-- God has numbered your kingdom and put an end to it. 'TEKEL' means you have been weighed on the scales and found deficient. 'PERES' means your kingdom has been divided and given over to the Medes and Persians.}

The king is stunned. Can you imagine the desperation! He didn't have long to be in suspense.

Daniel 5:30.31-{That same night Belshazzer the Chaldean king was slain. So Darius the Mede received the kingdom at about the age of sixty-two.} "Crownless and Scepterless, Belshazzer lay-a robe of purple 'round a form of clay."

There we have it. The two-winged lion was dead. The year 538 B.C. Medo-Persia under Darius had taken over night on schedule! The bear Daniel saw in dream had conquered the world!

How is the "beast" of Rev. 13 like Medo-Persia?

The Medo-Persians had a rule that once they made a law-it stuck, and could never be reversed. The government was considered infallible. You will see shortly that the "beast takes this same policy. Medo-Persia ruled until the empire met up with a young man whose military genius was uncanny- Alexander the Great. He became a great ruler at the age of 25!

It was October 1, 331 B.C. At the head of his armies Alexander met the Persian forces head on and defeated them in the battle of Arbela. His military genius made Greece to emerge as the third world empire. The Leopard with four heads and four wings of Danielsvision had replaced the Medo-Persian bear.

But why the four heads?

Alexander had conquered the world. But he could not conquer himself. At a drunken debauch he drank the Herculean cup full of alcohol. It was a huge thing. The human stomach can hardly hold more than a quart.

Of all horrors, he drank it twice! And it killed him dead.

Alexander died with a raging fever at the age of 33. The year was 323 B.C. His will declared that the kingdom should go "to the strongest." His four generals, Cassander, Lysimachus, Seleuchus and Ptolomy took over the empire and divided it into four parts.

These divisions are represented by the four heads of the leopard beast. What are the four wings? They represent swiftness. Greece had conquered the world in only 13 years. Such a feat has never been equaled.

Before his death, Alexander had ordered the Greek cities to worship him as god. The "beast" of Rev. 13 is "like unto a leopard" because it took the Greek culture and also has a leader that claims worship as God.

Who is the "terrible" beast of Daniel 7?

Daniel 7:7.23-{After this I kept looking in the night visions, and behold, a fourth beast, dreadful and terrifying and extremely strong; and it had large iron teeth. It devoured and crushed, and trampled down the remainder with its feet, and it was different from all the beasts that were before it, and had ten horns.} Thus, he said: 'the fourth beast will be a fourth kingdom on the earth, which will be different from all the other kingdoms, and it will devour the whole earth and tread it down and crush it.

The fourth kingdom, represented by this terrible beast is Rome. Rome conquered Greece in 168 B.C. and eventually gave its power to the beast of Rev. 13. Out of the fourth "terrible beast" comes a "little horn."

Now here is something amazing. The beast of Rev. 13 and the little horn of Daniel 7 are the one and the same power! God wants to make sure that there is no mistaking who this power is, so He describes it in both prophetic books.

Isn't Bible prophecy fantastic! Look at the description of the "little horn."

Daniel 7:8.24.25-{While I was contemplating the horns, behold, another horn, a little one, came up among them, and three of the first horns were pulled out by the roots before it; and behold, this horn possessed eyes like the eyes of a man, and a mouth uttering great boasts. As for the ten horns, out of this kingdom ten kings will arise; and another will arise after them, and he will be different from, the previous ones and will subdue three kings. And he will speak against the Most High and wear down the saints of the Highest One, and he will intend to make alterations in times of the law; and they will be given into his hand for a time, times, and a half a time.}

If you compare this description of the "little horn" with the description of the "beast" of Rev.13, you will see that they are one and the same power. One of the most startling things about this power is that it would "think to change times and laws." Daniel 7:25. Here is a man that sets himself up as equal with God, and dares to tamper with His law-the constitution of the universe! With blasphemous audacity he does his work. But God has said, "All His commandments are sure." Ps. 111:7.8-{The works of His hands are truth and justice; All His precepts are sure. They are upheld forever and ever; They are performed in truth and uprightness.}

The next clue to identify the beast, is the time period which God gives for its reign before it receives its "deadly wound." It would reign for 1260 years. Just so there is no mistake on this, He repeats this period seven times in Daniel and Rev. Now-just one more clue before I tell you who the beast is. It's not only the same as the "little horn" of Daniel 7, but it is also the power as the great whore riding upon the scarlet colored beast of Rev 17. Watch closely.

Rev.17:1-3- {And one of the seven angels who had the seven bowls came and spoke with me, saying, "Come here, I shall show you the judgment of the great harlot who sits upon many waters, with whom the kings of the earth committed acts of immorality, and those who dwell on the earth were made drunk with the wine of her immorality." And he carried me away in the spirit into the wilderness; and I saw a woman sitting on a scarlet beast, full of blasphemous names, having seven heads and ten horns.}

There are those heads and horns again. We have come to associate them with Rome. The Harlot is controlling Rome-riding it around-making her seat on it. Familiar isn't it! Now it gets even clearer.

This "Harlot" represents a corrupt church system. And get this-Rev.17:4-{And the woman was clothed in purple and scarlet, and adorned with gold and precious stones and pearls, having in her hand a gold cup full of abominations and of the unclean things of her immorality.} It is a rich church.

A woman in Bible prophecy represents a church. God likens His people to a "comely and delicate woman." Jeremiah 6:2. A virgin is God's pure church. A harlot (whore) is a corrupt church.

Right here in verse 5 she's called a Harlot. Rev.17:5-{And upon her forehead a name was written, a mystery, "BABYLON THE GREAT, THE MOTHER OF HARLOTS AND OF THE ABOMINATIONS OF THE EARTH."} It is not only a church, it is a mother church. It is a world power. But get this- Rev.17:6 {And I saw the woman drunk with the blood of the saints, and with the blood of the witnesses of Jesus. And when I saw her, I wondered greatly.} Oh yes! She kills people. She has killed God's people before and she will kill God's people again.

Amazing! Why would our heavenly Father who is so loving and kind talk about a church, of all things, and expose it to the world? Why does He who is so full of pity and love warn anyone who even follows this power and receives its mark that they will end up in the lake of fire?

The answer is because it is true. Though God is very tenderhearted, He always tells the truth.

I know it is shocking, but here is a corrupt church power that Satan has used to deceive the whole world and rob men and women of their eternal life by using deception. Like Nimrod and Alexander the Great, this power has leaders who divert the attention and worship of the people from the true, living God, to themselves. These leaders turn people from heeding the word of God to heeding their word; from obeying the commandments of God, to obeying their commandments. This is why God tells it like it is-because He is love.

And remember, there are many sincere, lovely Christians in this fallen church named "Babylon," and they will hear God's call and come out.

Look at this! Rev.18:2.4.5- {And he cried out with a mighty voice, saying, "Fallen, fallen is Babylon the great! And she has become a dwelling place of demons and a prison of every unclean spirit, and a prison of every unclean and hateful bird." And I heard another voice from heaven saying, "Come out of her, my people, that you may not participate in her sins and that you may not receive of her plagues; for her sins have piled up (joined together) as high as heaven, and God has remembered her iniquities."}

Now- who is this "beast?" What power-
(1) Received its "seat" and authority from Rome. Rev.13:4.
(2) Rules the world for 1260 years (from 538A.D.-1798 A.D.)
(3) Then received a "deadly wound" which later heals.Rev.13:3

(4) Is both a political and a religious power, which is worshiped Rev.13:4.
(5) Tampered with God's law. Daniel 7:25
(6) Has a leader who claims to be God on the earth and to be able to forgive sins (blasphemy) Rev.13:1.
(7) Is a mother church (daughters have come out of her). Rev. 17:5.
(8) Made war with the saints. Rev.13:7
(9) Is a world power which is wondered at. Rev.13:3.4.
(10) Has a "man" at the head of it with the number of his name being 666. Rev.13:18.
(11) Has a dreaded "mark" which will cause you, if any person, to be cast into the lake of fire and lose eternal life. Rev. 14:9.10.

By now, most of the people have guessed that it is the Papacy. They are correct. It is the only power on the face of the earth that fits all the Bible characteristics for it.

THE BEAST DESCRIBED

Let's take a close look at this thing to make sure there is no mistake.

Rev.13:2-{And the beast which I saw was like a leopard, and his feet were like those of a bear, and his mouth like the mouth of a lion. And the dragon gave him his power and his throne and great authority.}

Emperor Justinian "gave" the power of Rome to the pope when he decreed that the pope should be over all the Christian churches of the earth. The Papacy was established in 538 A.D., when the Emperor's general Belisarius drove the Ostrogoths from Rome. Rome gave him his "seat." Bible prophecy predicted it hundreds of years before it happened!

From 538 A.D. the Papacy ruled for exactly 1260 years, until 1798 when something incredible happened. The pope was taken prisoner! Napoleon's general, Berthier, captured the pope and took him to France! He later died.

A deadly wound. The Papacy had reigned exactly for 1260 years. Could it have just been a coincidence? Why did Berthier do it?

Napoleon wanted to rule the world. The Papacy stood in his way. I wonder if they knew they were fulfilling prophecy in spite of themselves!

Rev.13:3 {And I saw one of the heads as if it had been slain, and his fatal wound was healed. And the whole earth was amazed and followed after the beast.}

In 1929, the Italian government recognizes Vatican City as an independent state. Once again, the pope was king. On March 9, 1929, he said, "The peoples of the entire world are with us." The San Francisco Chronicle published an account of the pact signing on the front page of its newspaper. It actually read like this, "Mussolini and Gaspari Sign Historic Pact. Heal wound of Many Years." That is fantastic! The Bible predicted that its wound would be healed, and the newspaper confirmed it in the exact same words.

Though this great organization was not officially established until 538 A.D., the apostle Paul saw forces at work that were preparing the way. What was going on back there that he could have seen? Here is what happened.

After Jesus went back to heaven, the early church grew rapidly under the blessing of the Holy Spirit. Jesus had predicted the treatment that His people were to receive. Matt.24:9-{"Then they will deliver you to tribulation, and will kill you, and you will be hated by all nations on account of my name."}

This was literally fulfilled. Look at this amazing account. "Their execution was made into a game," wrote Tacitus describing the persecutions under Nero. "They were covered with the skins of wild animals and torn to pieces by dogs. They were hung on crosses. They were burned, wrapped in flammable material and set on fire, to illuminate the night. "To escape death, they had but to repudiate Christ and sacrifice to the emperor." Some did, but many more were tortured to death rather than deny their Lord.

"Paganism foresaw that should the gospel triumph, her temples and altars would be swept away; therefore she summoned her forces to destroy Christianity. Christians were stripped of their possessions and driven from their homes. Great numbers sealed their testimony with their blood. Noble and slave, rich and poor, learned and ignorant, were alike slain without mercy.

"Beneath the hills outside the city of Rome, long galleries had been through earth and rock; the dark and intricate network of passages extended for miles beyond the city walls. In these underground retreats the followers of Christ buried their dead; and here also, when suspected, they found a home."

Heb.11;35-{Women received back their dead by resurrection; and others were tortured, not accepting their release, in order that they might obtain a better resurrection} They rejoiced that they were accounted worthy to suffer for the truth, and songs of triumph ascended from the midst of the crackling flames.

Satan could not wipe them out. For years emperors Nero and Diocletian slaughtered them by the thousands.

"You may kill us, condemn us." said one Christian to his persecutors, "your injustice is the proof that we are innocent."

Until 313 A.D. it was against the law to be a Christian. Such a person was an automatic criminal. But the followers of Jesus spread everywhere.

Satan could see that he had to change tactics. He would come up with a better scheme. What could the devil think of to do that would be better than killing Christians? Make things easy- and infiltrate! Like a wise general he would corrupt the church from the inside!

Watch what happens. A great shout goes up in the empire. Emperor Constantine has become a Christian! The Christians are euphoric. No more being torn apart by dogs and lions, or used as dupes to be cut down in cold blood, or human torches to light up the arena for the gladiators. Now Christianity is the state religion!

Things are going great. Or so it seems.

But little by little, as everyone relaxes and quits worrying about being tortured to death, something happens. Compromise! Gradually the leaders, for the sake of popularity and gain let down the standards to make it easier for the pagans to come into the church. But this brings in errors and pagan customs.

Not all surprised by Satan's scheme to corrupt His church from within. God gives us fair warning. Listen to Paul's shocking words.

2Thess. 2:1-4.7-{Now we request you, brethren, with regard to the coming of our Lord Jesus Christ, and our gathering to Him, that you may not be quickly shaken from your composure or be disturbed either by a spirit or a message or a letter as if from us, to the effect that the day of the Lord has come. Let no one in any way deceive you, for it will not come unless the apostasy comes first, and the man of lawlessness is revealed, the son of destruction, who opposes and exalts himself above every so-called god or object of worship, so that he takes his seat in the temple of God, displaying himself as God, for the mystery of lawlessness is already at work; only he who now restrains will do so until he is taking out of the way.}

Oh Yes! He saw it coming. The mysterious work of corruption rapidly progressed after the death of the last apostle.

Question: what happened?

After persecution ceased, Satan's great device was to control the leaders of the church. If he could inflate their ego; make them money hungry, the whole body would be affected. A popularity contest would be on to get as many heathen to accept Christianity as possible. The wealth and prestige of the church would grow. Who cares if you have to change the Bible somewhat to get them! Just introduce some of the heathen customs and rites into Christianity, give them Christian names, and the heathen will flock in.

Of all horrors that is just what happened!

Satanic apostles had gone throughout the empire region establishing churches in many cities. As time went by, smaller churches were built in the surrounding country-sides. The larger churches were in Jerusalem, Rome, and Alexandra, Egypt. Rome finally emerged on top. The next step in the plot was for church leaders to get control of the state, to help enforce their decrees. They achieved this beyond their wildest dreams. The epitome of this came when in 538 A.D. the entire city of Rome was handed over to the pope the Bishop of Rome. For the next 1260 years, church leaders reigned with full civil authority.

All just as predicted in prophecy! Incredible! But look at this shocker.

Rev 13:1 says that the beast has "the name of blasphemy." This became one of the leading doctrines of the church that its visible head is invested with supreme authority over bishops and pastors in all parts of the world. More than this, he took the very name of God! He was addressed as "Lord God the Pope" and declared to be "infallible." He demands the worship of all men.

What about 666? Let's take a shocking look. On the pope's official mitre has been the title "Vicatius Filii Dei," which means, "Vicar of the Son of God."

The claim that this is his official title has been stated publicly through the years. This April 18, 1915 issue of Our Sunday Visitor, states: "The letters inscribed in the pope's mitre are these: 'VICARIUS FILII DEI,' which is Latin for Vicar of the Son of God." Rev. 13:18-Here is wisdom. Let him who has understanding calculate the number of the beast, for the number is that of a man; and his number is six hundred and sixty- six.

Let's do it now and see what we find. Remember the Roman numerals you learned in school?

V=5
I=1
C=100
A=0
R=0
I=1
U=5
S=0

F=0
I=1
L=50
I=1
I=1
D=500
E=0
I=1

Total = 666 IMPOSSIBLE BUT TRUE

I want to be quick to say that when a person shares this shocking revelation, he must be kind and tactful. We must let people know that God loves us all. The truth must be told-but always in kindness.

The 1260 years of the Papacy's rule are called the "dark ages." I am sure you have heard that expression before. The reason it was so dark is because the priests forbade anyone to read or even have a Bible! Satan had to get the Bibles away from the people in order to keep them in darkness and superstition. The people just did not know any better. There was a time when if you were caught with a Bible, you were dragged out of your home, hung on a pole, and burned alive in your yard! What John sees next is so unbelievable that he is stunned.

THE SATANIC CHURCH

Can you imagine Christians killing other Christians? This is a horrible thought.

Get this, Rev.13:7 {And it was given to him to make war with the saints and to over come them; and authority over every tribe and people and tongue and nation was given to him.}

Rev.17:6 {And I saw the woman drunken with the blood of the saints, and with the blood of the witnesses of Jesus. And when I saw her, I wondered greatly.}

What a picture! No wonder John was so amazed. A stack of books could hardly contain the accounts of the 50 million Christians put to death as "heretics." For possessing a Bible, for believing that people ought to be free to worship God according to their own conscious; for these and many other "crimes," men, women, and little children were tortured to death.

History comes through loud and clear that whole villages and towns were wiped off the map for not conforming to the state church and her leader.

"Dignitaries of the church studied, under Satan their master to invent means to cause the greatest possible torture and not the life of the victim. In many cases the infernal process was repeated to the utmost limit of human endurance, until nature gave up the struggle, and the sufferer hailed death as a sweet release."

Such was the fate of those who opposed the Church of Rome.

If given the opportunity in the U.S. she would do the same today against "heretics." Her boast is that she never changes. The rector of the Catholic Institute of Paris, H.M.A. Baudrillart, revealed the attitude of the church and her leaders toward prosecution. Watch closely.

When confronted with "heresy," he said, "she does not content herself with persuasion, arguments of an intellectual and moral order appear to her insufficient, and she has recourse to force, to corporeal punishment, to torture."

For a shocking account of how the Waldenses, Albegenses, Bohemians, and others were massacred or slowly and secretly murdered for their faith read your history books. Do your own research and then you come back and tell me.

The most outstanding story is the one of the Waldenses.

They were some of the few people who had copies of the Bible during the early years of the Papacy's reign. They saw that under the guidance of Pope and priest, multitudes were vainly endeavoring to obtain pardon by afflicting their bodies for the sin of their souls. Oppressed with a sense of sin, and haunted with the fear of God's avenging wrath, many suffered on, until exhausted nature gave way and without one ray or hope they sank into the tomb. The Waldenses longed to break to these starving souls the bread of life, to open to them the messages of peace in the promises of God, and to point them to Christ as the only hope of salvation.

The Savior was represented by the priests as to devoid of sympathy with man in his fallen state that the meditation of priests and saints must be invoked. The Waldenses longed to point these souls to Jesus as their compassionate, loving Savior, standing with outstretched arms, inviting all to come to Him with their burden of sin, and obtain pardon and peace.

With quivering lip and tearful eye did he, often on bended knees, open to others the precious promises that reveal the sinner's only hope. Especially was the repetition of these words eagerly desired: "The blood of Jesus Christ His Son cleanses us from all sin." 1John1:7.

Many were undeceived in regard to the claims of Rome. They saw how vain the meditation of men in behalf of the sinner is. The assurances of a Savior's love seemed too much for some of these poor tempest tossed souls to realize. So great was the relief which it brought, such a flood of light was shed upon them, that they seemed uttered: "Will God indeed accept my offering? Will He smile upon me? Will He pardon me? The answer was read: Matt. 11:28 {"Come unto Me, all who are weary and heavy-laden, and I will give you rest.}

Faith grasped the promise, and the glad response was heard: "No more long pilgrimages to make, no more painful journey's to holy shrines. I may come to Jesus just as I am, and He will not spurn my prayer. 'Thy sins be forgiven thee.' Mine, even mine,
may be forgiven!" (Praise God!)

There was a strange and solemn power in the words of Scripture that spoke directly to the hearts of those who were longing for the truth. It was the voice of God, and it carried conviction to those who heard.

In many cases the messenger of truth was seen no more. He had made his way to other lands, of he was wearing out his life in some unknown dungeon, or perhaps his bones were whitening on the spot where he had witnessed for the truth.

The Waldensian missionaries were invading the kingdom of Satan. The very existence of this people, holding the faith of the ancient church, was a constant testimony to Rome's apostasy, and excited the most bitter hatred and persecution. Their refusal to surrender the Scriptures was an offense that Rome could not tolerate. She determined to blot them from the earth.

Pope Innocent VIII ordered "That malicious and abominable sect of malignants," if they refuse to abjure, to be crushed like venomous snakes,"

No charge could be brought against their moral character. Their grand offense was that they would not worship God according to the pope. For this crime, every disgrace, insult, and torture that men or devils could invent was heaped upon them. They were hunted to death; yet their blood watered the seed sown, and it failed not of yielding fruit. Scattered over many lands it will be carried forward to the close of time by those who also are willing to suffer all things "for the word of God, and for the testimony of Jesus Christ."

Keep in mind that these atrocities happened long before we were born. But the warning against receiving the "mark of the beast" is certainly for us today. Soon, you will know what the beast's "mark" is.

As we have learned, this power would "think to change times and laws." Daniel 7:25 How could it possible do that? Since the heathen were used to worshiping the images, the church ripped out the second commandment which forbids image worship. They placed images in the churches! But instead of heathen gods, they simply used images of dead Christians! The people were taught that these were merely to help increase their learning and devotion. But the result was far different.

Scripture says that he would "think to change times and laws." Look at this shocking statement from an official decretal.

The Pope has power to change times, to abrogate laws, and to dispense with all things, even the precepts of Christ." Decretal, de Tranlatic Episcop.

This is totally unbelievable! This has to be not real! But God damn it, it is. The word pope should be spelled poop. This is poop. This makes my mouth fall open. My drawers are getting dirty. I was amazed that the official statement of the poopacy was nearly word for word quote from the Bible.

To make matters worse, they split the tenth commandment in two, and still called it ten. I guess its no wonder. I heard that the pope and his cronies are really devil worshippers in secret. This can only explain these things.

Satan had caused the second commandment to be ripped out. But he was not finished. The leaders changed the fourth one also!

The change of the fourth commandment was attempted gradually over a period of time so as not to arouse anyone. But the change is a master piece of Satan's work. Get ready for a shock.

The following mind-boggling statements were made by church authorities and are documented.

Question- "Have you any other way of proving that the church (Roman Catholic) has the power to institute festivals of precept?"

Answer- "Had she not such power, she could not have done that in which all modern religionist agree with her-she could not have substituted the observance of Sunday, the first say of the week, for the observance of Saturday, the seventh day, a change for which there is no Scriptural authority." A Doctrinal Catechism, by Stephen Keenan, pg.174.

This is God damned incredible! This is truly God damned blasphemous! They all should be run out of town and then stoned.

"The catholic church." Declared Cardinal Gibbons, "by virtue of her divine mission changed the day from Saturday to Sunday."

Devine mission my ass. A divine mission right out of hell!

Again the question was asked to them:

Question- "Which is the Sabbath day?"

Answer- "Saturday is the Sabbath day."
Question- "Why do we observe Sunday instead of Saturday?"
Answer- "We observe Sunday instead of Saturday because the Catholic church, in Council of Laodicea (A.D.364) transferred the solemnity from Saturday to Sunday." The convert's Catechism of Catholic Doctrine, pg. 50, third edition.

What does the fourth commandment actually say? Here it is:

Exodus 20:8-11 {"Remember the Sabbath day, and to keep it holy. Six days shalt thou labor, and do all thy work: But the seventh day is the Sabbath of the Lord thy God: in it thou shalt not do any work, thou, nor thy son, nor thy daughter, thy maidservant, nor thy cattle, nor thy stranger that is within thy gates: For in six days the Lord made heaven and earth, the sea, and all that is in them, and rested the seventh day; wherefore the Lord blessed the Sabbath day, and hollowed it."}

Do church authorities acknowledge that there is no command in the Bible for the sanctification of Sunday?

They do! Look at this-Catholic Cardinal Gibbons, in faith of our fathers, pg 111, said, "You may read the Bible from Genesis to Revelation, and you will not find a single line authorizing the sanctification, and you will not find a single line authorizing the sanctification of Sunday. The Scriptures enforce the religious observance of Saturday, day which we never sanctify."

This is stupendous! Totally amazing! I mean really! You see in the Cardinal Council of Trent (1545 A.D.), church leaders ruled that "tradition" is of as great authority as the Bible! What! Excuse me!

They believed that God had given them the authority any way they pleased. By "tradition" they meant human teachings. These people are devil worshipers all the way. The truth is Satan told them to change it. Since they are devil worshipers they did what he said.

They serve the lord of darkness. All hail to the dark lord. My father who art in hell. In you we will obey. Screw Jehovah! Who needs him?

Matt.15:9-{'But in vain they do worship me, teaching as doctrines the precepts of men.'"} Even Jesus agrees here.

Just as they brought images into the church to make it easier for the pagans to come in, they changed the Sabbath of the Bible for the same reason.

How did it all start?

The sun was the main god of the heathen even back as far as ancient Babylon. Since they worshiped the sun on Sunday, the compromising church leaders could see that if they changed from Saturday to Sunday, it would accomplish several things.

(1) It would separate them from the Jews who were hated by many Romans and who, along with Jesus, had been worshiping on the Saturday from the beginning (and still do today). Luke 4:16- {And He came to Nazareth, where He had been brought up; and as was His custom, He entered the synagogue on the Sabbath, and stood up and read.}

(2) It would make it much easier for the pagans to come into the church if the Christians met on the same day that the pagan world did. This is real sweet of them isn't it?

It worked well. Pagans flocked in by the thousands. Satan's plan of compromise was doing its baleful work. The change was attempted gradually, but many of the true hearted, loyal Christians were alarmed. They came to the leaders and wanted to know why they had dared tamper with the law of Almighty God! The church leaders knew this would happen-and they had an answer ready. It is a master piece. If a person does not know the Bible well it sounds good.

The people were told they were worshiping on Sunday now because Jesus rose from the dead on that day.

There is not even one verse in the Bible that tells us to do this, but that is what they were told. Amazing! Maybe you have even heard it your self! Many do not realize it, but in Romans 6:3-5 we see that it is baptism that represents the resurrection (coming up out of the water) to a new life in Christ-not the day of the sun.

When Emperor Constantine became a Christian, Christianity became the state religion you remember. As thousands of sunworshipers flocked into the church, it was not long before they had a dominating influence. Most of his top officials had been sunworshipers.

Because the Roman government was getting shaky, Constantine consulted with his aids and with church officials in Rome. "What shall we do? How can we unite and stabilize the government?"

The council of the church leaders was timely- "Pass a Sunday law. Force everyone to cease work and honor Sunday."

That was it! It would satisfy the sun-worshiping pagans, and unite the pagans, Christians, and the Roman Empire as never before!

The year is 321 A.D. Constantine, yielding to the suggestion of church leaders passes the first Sunday law! Here it is, straight out of record: "Let all the judges and town people, and the occupation of all trades rest on the venerable day of the sun." Edict of March 7, 321 A.D. Corpus Juris Civilis Cod,. Lib. 3,tit. 12, Lex. 3

The Christians who would not compromise and dishonor God found themselves in a dilemma. Satan had worked things around so that you were forced to honor the pagan "day of the sun" or pay the penalty. Even after the Emperor's Sunday law, many Christians continued to honor and keep holy the Seventh-day Sabbath that their Savior had kept. God knew what was going on and had predicted that the man of sin would "think to change times and laws." Satan was about to pull off a world-wide hoax.

Bibles were forbidden by the priests. As the years went by, the new generations (without Bibles) would forget all about the Sabbath of the Lord.

Not only that from time to time, great church councils were held. In nearly everyone, the Sabbath which God had given as a memorial of His creation of the world was pressed down, and Sunday was exalted. The pagan festival of Sunday finally came to be regarded as the "Lords day" (by pope Sylvester, 314-337 A.D.) and the church leaders pronounced the Bible Sabbath a relic of the Jews, and those who honored it(in obedience to the fourth commandment of God) were pronounced to be "accursed."

To rip out the commandment right in the center, put in Sunday worship as a counterfeit, take the Bibles away, and command the whole world to accept it-this was the king of all swindles!

You see, Satan hates the fourth commandment more than all others because it is the only one that tells who God really is-the creator of "Heaven and earth, and sea, and all that in them is." Exodus 20:11. You could worship any god and keep the other nine (not kill, steal, etc.) but to keep the fourth commandment you must worship the creator of the universe who Himself rested on the seventh day and commanded His people to do the same in a love relationship with Himself.

As the centuries went by, the people with no Bibles, forgot about God's Sabbath, and Sunday worship became firmly established. Many even today are ignorant on the subject.

The Waldenses which I have mentioned, and some other groups through the dark ages did secretly have Bibles, and many did keep the Bible Sabbath on Saturday like Jesus did-all through out history. But they were as outlaws. Whenever they were caught they were tortured to death. Their mangled corpses show the world the tactics that the beast has always used-force.

Of God's faithful in the last says it says, Rev.14:12-{Here is the perseverance of the saints who keep the commandments of God and their faith in Jesus.}

In modern times, leaders who know what they are talking about will admit that men changed the Sabbath and not God. Look at these startling statements from the Protestant leaders:

Methodist-"The reason we observe the first day instead of the seventh day is based on no positive command. One will search the Scriptures in vain for authority for changing from the seventh day to the first." Clovis G Chappell, Ten rules for living, pg. 61.

Baptist-Harold Lindsell, former editor of Christianity Today, said, "There is nothing in Scripture that requires us to keep Sunday rather than Saturday as a holy day," Christianity Today, November 5, 1976.

Episcopal-"The Bible commandment says on the seventh day thou shalt rest. That is Saturday. Nowhere in the Bible is it laid down that worship should be done on Sunday." Philip Carrington, Toronto Daily Star, October 26, 1949.

Our Catholic friends know how the change came about. They say, "we observe Sunday instead of Saturday because the Catholic church in the council of Laodicea, transferred the solemnity from Saturday to Sunday." The Converts Catechism of Catholic Doctrine, Third edition, pg. 50.

The Catholic Press said, "Sunday is a Catholic institution, and its claims to observation can be defended only on Catholic principles. From the beginning to end in Scripture there is not a single passage from the last day of the week to the first."

God speaks of the seventh day 126 times in the Old Testament and 62 times in the New Testament. The first day of the week is mentioned only eight times in the New Testament. A catholic priest offered $1000 to anyone who could find one Bible verse to indicate that Sunday is now holy and should be observed instead of the seventh day. No one responded. I have done the same, but received no response. Why not?

It says that the beast (little horn power) would "think to change times and laws." Daniel 7:25.

The second commandment was ripped out and images were brought in. The fourth commandment is the only one that deals with time. Look at this shocking announcement:

"The Pope has power to change times, to abrogate laws, and to dispense with all things, even the precepts of Christ. The Pope has the authority, and has often exercised it, to dispense with the command of Christ." Decretal, de Tranlatic Episcop. Cap.

Keep in mind that our God is kind and fair. Those who are keeping Sunday and breaking God's fourth commandment ignorantly are not under condemnation. Do not forget that. It is only those who know what God command's and willfully disobey who are committing sin. God's enemy knows that to break one of God's commandments is a sin which hurts our Savior and robs us of eternal life with Him if not repented of.

Satan laid this plot so deep that even many ministers are not aware of it. Many religious leaders are putting forth desperate efforts to keep facts on this subject away from the people.

Shocking but true, many ministers have not learned at school anything different than their teachers have learned before them. Then they teach their congregations what they learned from their teachers. It is perpetuated for generations. This is why even your own parents or grandparents may not have understood what God's word teaches about His seventh-day Sabbath. But when people honestly study the Bible for themselves- their eyes are opened.

Praise God! Many take their preachers word and just do not study God's word for themselves. Do you believe that?

I praise God that many millions of people around the world are learning these amazing truths about God's true Sabbath of the Bible and are starting to keep it holy in loving obedience to the Savior who died to redeem them.

As you begin to keep God's Sabbath holy, it becomes a delight. Sweet peace and joy fill your heart. You know that now you are not violating any of His loving commandments but are walking more closely with the Savior. Revelation 14:12 describes the faithful in the last says who "keep the commandments of God and the faith of Jesus."

The devil has been trying to get preachers to say that God's Ten Commandments have been done away with. But when will it ever be right to break God's sixth, eighth, of ninth commandments to kill, steal or lie? All ten stand do fall together because it is a sweet love relationship between you and God. In James 2:10.11

God says that if you break one, you break them all. It is like two lovers- it is either all or nothing.

The lovely Jesus said, Matt. 5:17.18 {"Do not think that I came to abolish the Law or the prophets; I did not come to abolish, but to fulfill. For truly, I say to you, until heaven and earth pass away, not the smallest letter of stroke shall pass away from the Law, until all is accomplished."} Heaven and earth have not passed away yet.

We are saved by God's grace and not by our obedience Eph.2:8 {For by grace you have been saved through faith; and that not of your selves, it is the gift of God;}His salvation is a free gift which we can receive by simple faith. But it is also true that is a person willfully, persistently disobeys God, it shows that he really does not love God enough to obey Him, and has not received this free gift. He has not been born again. God's true people will be obedient, happy people who love Him so much that they would rather die than sin against Him any more! Obedience becomes a joy when you are walking with Jesus Christ!

It is not new that many people that Moses received more than one sect of laws. On one trip up the mountain, God gave him the Ten Commandments which He says will stand forever. At another time, Moses received the ceremonial law. This law regulated the killing of animals. It was "added because of sin" and pointed forward to the sacrifice of the Son of God on the cross. It was to keep fresh In the people's minds that some day the real sacrifice for sin would come. Jesus is the innocent little lamb here.

John 1:29 {The next day he saw Jesus coming to him and said, "Behold, the Lamb of God who takes away the sin of the world!"}

Since Jesus really came and died for us, it is easy to see that God does not require us to kill animals any more. Aren't you glad?

There was another set of laws God gave to His people. They were the health laws found in Leviticus 11, and Deuteronomy

14. Because of these, God's people were the healthiest people in the world! They didn't get the horrible diseases of the other nations, or even like we have in our world today. Since our stomachs and bodies are the same as theirs, those who follow these wise and scientific health laws today also reap the delightful benefits. They just don't get this terrifying cancer, heart attacks, etc. like others.

Our God is so kind! It makes you fall in love with that lovely person named Jesus.

It was the ceremonial Law of Moses that was done away with on the cross. This law had animal sacrifices meat and drink offerings, and seven ceremonial Sabbaths that rotated through the year and fell on various days of the week.

The ceremonial law pointed torward to the death of dear Jesus on the cross, and it not required of us now. These ceremonial meat and drink offerings, new moons and Sabbath days were a "shadow of things to come; but the body is of Christ."

Col.2:16.17-{Therefore let no one act as your judge in regard to food or drink or in respect to a festival or a new moon or a Sabbath day- things which are a mere shadow of what is to come; but the substance belongs to Christ.} They were all a "shadow" of the cross. Paul calls it the "handwriting of ordinances" and makes it clear that it was nailed to "His cross." Col.2:14-{having canceled out the certificate of debt consisting of decrees against us and which was hostile to us; and He has taken it out of the way, having nailed it to the cross.}

The seven ceremonial Sabbaths that rotated through the year are not required of us now, and we were totally separate from the "Sabbath of the Lord" that came every week. Not only does God want his people to observe His weekly Sabbath here on earth in a happy relationship with Himself, but the Bible says that we will still be keeping it even with heaven! Isaiah 66:22.23-{"For just as the new heavens and the new earth Which I make will endure before Me." Declares the Lord. "So your offspring and your name will endure. And it shall be from new moon to new moon And from Sabbath to Sabbath, All mankind will come to bow down before Me," says the Lord.}

Satan has palmed off the biggest counterfeit in the history of man!

Look at this shocker- The Catholic authorities proclaim: "The Bible says, 'Remember that thou keep holy the Sabbath day.'"

The Catholic church says, 'No! By my divine power I abolish the Sabbath day, and command you to keep the first day of the week.'

"And lo, the whole civilized world bows down in reverent obedience to the command of the holy Catholic Church!" Father Enright, C.S.S.R. of the Redemptoral College, Kansas City, Mo., as taken from History of the Sabbath, pg.802.

Amazing and true! No wonder the Bible says: {And they worshiped the dragon, because he gave his authority to the beast; and they worshiped the beast, saying, "Who is like the beast, and who is able to wage war with him?" And all who dwell on the earth will worship him, everyone whose name has not been written from the foundation of the world in the book of life of the Lamb who has been slain.}

Incredible! No time has been lost track of. Some ministers who do not have one Bible text will say, "Do not worry about God's commandments, just worship God every day, or pick one day in seven." Some highly educated ministers have even said, "Do not worry about following the Bible, it is out of date. You just live a good life and everything will be alright."

Many ministers, when asked, will honestly say, "I know that Saturday is the seventh day Sabbath of the Bible, and God has not changed it, but if I were to tell the people that, I would lose my job!"

But it was fear of losing his job and getting in trouble that caused Pilate to do what he did! Remember? When the people shouted, "If thou let this man go, thou art not Caesar's friend" John 19:12. Pilate was scared. If people turned against him for letting Jesus go, no telling what might happen. It would cost him his job!

The record says, "Mark 15:15-{And wishing to satisfy the multitude, Pilate released Barabbas for them, and after having Jesus scourged, he delivered Him to be crucified.} That is heavy!

Again I say no marvel that the world wonders after and worships the beast-no marvel! To save their jobs or to save their necks people compromise. I praise God that many who are learning these truths are honest enough to come back to the Bible and follow Jesus all the way home. God makes it so plain-even a child can understand. Only those who love our heavenly Father and His dear Son with all their hearts, will stand through the last days and not worship the beast of receive his "mark." By the way-the dreaded "mark of the beast"-what is it? Get ready for a shock.

THE MARK OF THE BEAST

The "Mark of the Beast" and the Seal of God are direct opposites. In the end, everyone will have one or the other. Those who choose the seal of God will be with Jesus in His wonderful kingdom-that gorgeous paradise of beauty beyond our wildest dreams. It is a land where love, peace, and happiness reign. Those who choose the mark of the beast will be cast into the lake of fire.

Man! If there isn't anything we don't want- it is the mark of the beast!

Now we are ready to discover the hoax of all hoaxes. The counterfeit that will deceive the whole world and plunge it into eternal despair is about to unfold. It will be "the straw that broke the camel's back." Listen to what God has to say about this dreaded "mark." Rev.14:9.10-{And another angel, a third one, followed them, saying with a loud voice, "If anyone worships the beast and his image, and receives a mark on his forehead or upon his hand, he also will drink of the wine of the wrath of God, which is mixed in full strength in the cup of His anger; and he will be tormented with fire and brimstone in the presence of the holy angels and in the presence of the Lamb."}

There are two easy ways to learn what the mark of the best is.
(1) Ask the beast what the mark of its authority is. It will tell you quite frankly.
(2) Find what the "seal of God" is, and you will know that the "mark of the beast" is just the opposite.

The reason why such a terrible warning is given against receiving this "mark" is because; to receive it is a great sin against God. The issue will be a test for the entire world.

On the other hand, those who choose the seal of God will be showing their love and loyalty to Him instead of to the beast- even in the face of death!

In the verse below, the Bible reveals that pressure will be applied by the image of the beast. Those who refuse the beast's mark will be persecuted, boycotted, not allowed to buy or sell, and finally sentenced to death! Watch closely.

Rev.13:15.17-{And there was given to him to give breath to the image of the beast, that the image of the beast might even speak and cause as many as do not worship the image of the beast to be killed. and he provides that no one should be able to buy or sell, except the one who has the mark, either the name of the beast or the number of his name.}

What a picture! No matter which way you look at it, a crisis is stealing upon this world! People can feel it. And it will not be long. Those who love God with all their hearts will not conform to the pressure whatever comes our way. We will become martyrs for Christ. Imagine having the opportunity to become a martyr for Christ. We will certainly have a better resurrection for eternity. We will stand firm in the face of death, and receive the seal of the living God in our foreheads. This will be our choice. Is it your choice? It is no trivial thing. This is a matter of life or death. This is also a matter of eternal life or eternal death. Concerning God's seal it says: Rev.7:2.3-{And I saw another angel ascending from the rising sun, having the seal of the living

God; and he cried out with a loud voice to the four angels to whom it was granted to harm the earth and the sea, saying, "Do not harm the earth or the sea or the trees, until we have sealed the bond-servants of our God on their foreheads."}

"Winds" in prophecy stand for strife and war. A global war is coming, as we will soon see. But here, the angels are holding it back until the servants of God can have a chance to receive his seal.

It would have all broken loose before now but God in His great love and mercy, is holding it back just for a little while longer. And there have been "smoke screens." Nations have been talking "peace" while preparing for "high tech" war. "Peace, peace" is cried, when "there is no peace." It is no accident that the "mark of the beast" has not yet been enforced. But soon the angels will start to let loose! Whether it is by T.V., or radio, internet, or by seeing the persecution of others in the courts who have God's seal; people will learn the difference between the "seal" and the "mark" and will take their stand. This very book may be one method God has chosen for you to learn these fantastic truths! It is no coincidence that you are reading this book now. God is waiting for the sincere, humble followers of Jesus Christ to learn the great issues that are involver here! That is to choose which one the seal of God or the mark of the beast. Satan has done everything to deceive you up to this point. This little book is revealing this fact to you right now.

When we learn all of the issues that are involved here, then we will make a final decision because we have to. Then the curtains will close! Its closing time! Then there will come the close of probation for the human race. What comes next are the seven last plagues, and the earths last, stupendous battle. (We will look at these things in a minute) Where you stand then determines the choices you make right now! Are you ready to make the right God damned choice or the God blessed choice? CHOOSE.

First of all, what is God's "seal?" A seal is something having to do with the legal affairs. A law is stamped with the seal of the ruling government. A seal has three parts:

(1) The name of the ruler.
(2) The ruler's title.
(3) The territory over which he rules.

When the government seal is on a law, or on currency, it is official. The whole loyal nation stand's behind it. God's seal makes His law official, and the whole loyal universe stands behind it.

Anyone disloyal to the seal of the government, and to the law upon which it is attached, is looked upon as being disloyal to the government itself. Just as a government ruler's seal is placed in his law to make it official, God's seal is in His law. Here is what God says: Isaiah 8:16-{Bind up the testimony, deal the law among my disciples.}

Where are we sealed? We are in the forehead. His law is in our hearts. Under the new covenant, His promise is: Heb. 10:16-{"This is the covenant that I will make with them after those days, say the Lord: I will put My laws upon their heart, And upon their mind I will write them,"}

The Holy Spirit places the seal of God in our foreheads when we choose it. The forehead contains the "frontal lobe." This section of the brain is where our conscience is. When you receive the seal of God in your forehead, it means you have it in your conscience. You believe in it. You are loyal to it.

Just as the government ruler uses his "seal" to enforce His law. The beast will use his seal (mark) to try to enforce his law in place of God's law.

Where will you find the seal of God with its three parts? You will find it in the very center of His law. Take a look: Exodus 20:8-11-{Remember the Sabbath day, to keep it holy. Six days, you shall labor and do all your work, but the seventh day is a Sabbath of the Lord your God; in it you shall not do any work, you or your son or your daughter, your male or your female servant or your cattle or your sojourner who stays with you. For in six days the Lord made the heavens and the earth, the sea and all that is in them, and rested on the seventh day; therefore the Lord blessed the Sabbath day and made it holy.}

This is the only place in the Bible where you will find God's seal. Here are the three part seal:

(1) His name-"The Lord."
(2) His title-"Thy God." (Creator)
(3) His Territory-"heaven and earth, and sea, and all that is in them is."

This is fantastic! No wonder Satan has worked so hard to hide the truth of the sacred Sabbath from us. It is God's sign!

You may ask "Is the Sabbath really the seal of God?" Let's look in Ezekiel 20:12.20-{And also I gave them My Sabbaths to be a sign between Me and them, that they might know that I am the Lord, who sanctifies them. And sanctify My Sabbaths; and they shall be a sign between Me and you, that you may know that I am the Lord your God.} The word "sign" means the same as "seal." Rom.4:11-{and he received the sign of circumcision, a seal of the righteousness of the faith which he had while uncircumcised, that he might be the father of all who believe without being circumcised, that righteousness might be reckoned to them.} What could be clearer? The seal of God is His Sabbath.

Satan knew that he had to get at this very part. No wonder the "beast" of Revelation ripped it out and put in a substitute! Look at this shocking statement concerning the beast's terrible act. "Of course the Catholic Church claims that the ecclesiastical power and authority in religious matters." Sunday worship is the mark of the Papacy's authority. The "mark." Sunday worship is the 'mark of the beast!"

The issues are plain. God says that He is the true God. He has given His Sabbath as a sign of His authority as the creator of all. By keeping it, we recognize His authority. But the Catholic Church says in effect, "No! Keep the first day of the week, and lo, the entire civilized world bows in reverent obedience to the command of the holy Catholic Church." It is the GOD

DAMNED MARK OF THE BEAST. It's the mark of our authority to over rule Gods law.

But what about our loved ones who are keeping Sunday and don't know any better? Do they have the mark of the beast?

No! No! No! Only those who know better and realize that they are breaking God's fourth commandment are held accountable.

The Bible says in James 4:17-{Therefore, to no one who knows the right thing to do, and does not do it, to him it is sin.} You and I now are held accountable. Soon all will know. God is making this very point a great test for the world in the last days. It will separate those who really love God enough to obey Him, (even amid persecution) from those who merely claim to be Christians, but like Pilate, will compromise, go along with the crowd and end up with the mark of the beast. The "Mark" will not officially be received until it is enforced by the "two horned beast" of Revelation 13.

We certainly do not want to hurt our loving Savior by breaking any of His commandments. That would break His heart. Sin hurts Him most of all. He suffered agony on the cross to take away our sins. Blood ran from His holy body. His love for us is very tender. Those who willfully receive the mark of the beast are willing to hurt the loving heart of God. As we choose to keep all of His commandments, it makes Him glad.

As you begin to keep His seventh day Sabbath holy, He will make it the happiest day of the week for you. You will be able to lay aside your cares and labors one whole day and have a beautiful rest with Jesus not only physically, but a rest of soul, a joyful peace and freedom from guilt.

If you are working in your job on God's Sabbath now, He will help you with that too. I have never seen it fail. Those who determine to keep His Sabbath holy and not work on Saturday have God's special care and miraculous providence. He will either help you get the Sabbath off from work, or if you have to lose your job, he will give you a better one! I guarantee it. That is God's love!

That is our kind Heavenly Father.

People in every nation will be tested on this very point. Millions around the world have discovered these amazing truths just like you have, and are rejoicing in a closer walk with Jesus than ever before.

Here is another question. What does it mean to receive the mark in your hand?

Remember, to receive it in the forehead means that you believe in it, you are loyal to it. There will also be an outward sign of some kind where by people will be able to tell who has the mark and who does not. We will get to that here shortly. To receive it in the hand means that when the mark is enforced by the "image of the beast," they go along with it, not because they believe in it, but just to be able to buy and sell. They will also try to keep their jobs, and save their lives. The hand is a symbol of work and making a living.

This is a shocking thought! How could anything like that happen in our free country! If the "image of the beast" tries to enforce everyone to receive the "mark of the beast." how does he do it?

Who is the "image of the beast" anyway?

THE IMAGE OF THE BEAST

Who is the "image of the beast?"
What does it do?
Who gives it power?

It gets more explosive as we go. It is all in Revelation 13. Here is the picture: Rev.13:11.12.15-17{And I saw another beast coming up out of the earth; and he had two horns like a lamb, and he spoke as a dragon. And he exercises all the authority of the first beast in his presence. And he makes the earth and those who dwell in it to worship the beast, whose fatal wound was healed. And there was given to him to give breath to the image of the beast, that the image of the beast might even speak and cause as many as do not worship the image of the beast to be killed. And he causes all, the small and the great, and the rich and the poor, and the free men and the slaves, to be given a mark of their fight hand, or on their forehead, and he provides that no one should be able to buy or to sell, except the one who has the mark, either the name of the beast or the number of his name.}

What a picture! Even though it seems impossible, God's word says it will happen.

First let me say that I love my country. I have spent time on foreign soil serving my country. I have worn the uniform. I am glad I live in the United States. But this is what God's word has to say.

The United States (the two horned beast), will cause all to worship the first beast by enforcing the "mark" of the beast law! The word "cause" in the original Greek means "force." A national Sunday law will be enforced in our country. In chapter one, we have already seen that it is coming and some of the reasons why.

We have already learned that. (1) The "two horned beast" is the United States. (2) The first beast is the Papacy. The "image of the beast" is a religious power much like the Papacy (in the U.S.), teaching many of the same false teachings. The "image" of the beast is the majority of the Protestant world. To say it plainly, Revelation 13 is revealing to us the astonishing fact that "Protestant America" will cause all to worship the Papacy and receive its "mark" by passing a national Sunday law, and that all who do not go along with it will suffer the consequences!

When man reaches the depth of spiritual decay and passes that law, it will not only make an "image" to the beast in our country and copy the old papal principle of persecution, it will set up the procedure for all to receive the "mark of the beast!"

It is coming clear! You see, it will not be the beast which enforces it's "mark" by law in our country, it will be its "image" which is Protestant America.

It all boils down to being forced to either obey the laws of our beloved country and disobey God, or having to violate the laws of the land in order to obey our Lord. That is a real test! If you are faithful and true to God, you will find yourself without a job, without the right to buy or to sell, and even under death penalty!

Does this sound impossible? It is already in progress! Large religious groups such as the Lords Day alliance want it, and already have articles in print concerning it. Is the principle of "separation of church and state" crumbling? The national Catholic journal, Catholic Twin Circle, said "All Americans would do well to petition the President and the Congress to make Federal law an amendment to the Constitution if need be to re-establish the Sabbath (meaning Sunday) as a national day of rest.

These powerful groups have genuine concerns. They are working for good things like better T.V. programs, to save the family, etc. But what they do not realize is that when the U.S. actually passes a national Sunday law, it has taken away the religious freedom of those who choose to keep God's day instead of the day of the sun worship, it is enforcing the "mark of the beast!" Those who go along with this oppressive law while knowing what they are doing will most definitely receive the "mark of the beast." Why? Because they will be disobeying the commandment of God in order to obey the tradition of men, Jesus said, Mark 7:7 {"In vain do they worship me, teaching for doctrine the commandments of men.}

Do not get me wrong, I do love my country. I am just sharing the facts. Please do not shoot the messenger.

If your head is still spinning at the shock of a future nationwide Sunday law and persecution in our country, all I can say is draw close to God! Draw closer than you have ever been before in your life. Fill your mind with the Bible instead of the T.V. and a thousand other things! Pray like you have never prayed before. He will help you! These things are coming with swift surety.

Believe it or not. In Virginia it is already been done. I mean a mandatory Sunday law along with the death sentence.

Get this shocking quote. In 1610, the First Sunday law in America, in Virginia required: "Every man and woman shall repair in the mourning to divine service and sermons preached upon the Sabbath (Sunday), and in the afternoon to divine service, and catechizing, upon pain for the first fault to lose their provision and the allowance for the whole week following; for the second, to lose said allowance and also be whipped; and for the third to suffer death!!! Laws and orders, Divine, Politique, and Martial, for the Colony in Virginia: first established by Sir Thomas Gates, knight Lieutenant General, the 24th of May, 1610.

Did you know that Sunday blue laws are still on the books in Virginia and other states?

It is "unconstitutional," said one lawyer living in Richmond, Va. (speaking of the Sunday law). "It is a religious law and it is unconstitutional." But it is still there!

Most states have had these "Sunday blue laws" enforced on and off throughout the last two hundred years. They come and go.

Many lie dormant just waiting.

Can you get a better picture at what is going on here? God knows what He is talking about and has given us fair warning. God's warning is a warning of love.

I.D. cards, numbers or something like this will allow the followers of the national Sunday law to buy and sell. They will have these "temporary" benefits. Tremendous pressure will be on to conform.

Terrorism and crime will be major factors. They are shooting out of control. People are scared. People are angry at these horrors and these things are helping bring back the death sentence. The Bible in many places pronounces the death sentence for the crimes of murder, rape, witchcraft, homosexuality, etc. (Genesis 9:5.6; Deuteronomy 22:25-29; Leviticus 20:13; Exodus 22:18). Last year less than 1100 people were executed now that number is 1500! Public opinion, only recently against capital punishment, now favors it two to one.

According to Bible prophecy it will come back.

Of all horrors! It will come back and be used against those who love and obey God! Rev. 13:15-{And there was given to him to give breath to the image of the beast, that the image of the beast might even speak and cause many as do not worship the image of the beast to be killed.}

Just a few days ago on the rainy streets of Eugene, OR I talked to a man on the street corner who had a Bible in one hand. I asked him if he was worshiping this day (Saturday) He said yes! I then asked him what would you do if they made you worship on Sunday and it would cost you your life. "He said they could have his life it was not worth a hill of beans anyway."

Do people know what is going on? Of course they don't, that is why I am writing this book.

To use force is to use the methods of the "dragon."

The second reason the Sunday law has been urged is the economic crises. You are so aware of the situation, so I do not even have to comment on it.

The third reason is, that religious leaders of all people will stir up the nation for this law which they will make people think is so needful. As stated in Chapter one, already media messages and articles have circulating all over the country urging the populace that "There will be no relief from mounting economic disaster until Sunday is strictly enforced by government decrees and action.

Now you and I can see clearly that this fulfillment of prophecy, urging the nation to enforce the "mark of the beast!" But to the average person who knows almost nothing about the Bible, this plea sounds pretty good.

Another thing that will help it come is miracles. Have you noticed the tremendous surge of interest in the supernatural lately?

God is certainly a God of miracles. And because of this, many believe that all miracles are from God. Not knowing their Bibles, they will be the more easily fooled by Satan's miracles,

Get this. Rev. 16:13.14-{And I saw coming out of the mouth of the dragon and out of the mouth of the beast and out of the mouth of the false prophet, three unclean spirits like frogs. for they are spirits of demons, performing signs, which go out to the kings of the whole world, to gather them together for the war of the great day of God, the Almighty.}

The point here is that the devils work miracles as well as God. By this deceptive means, the whole world will be deceived into worshiping the beast and receiving its mark. Through miracles, and Satan's angels appearing as dead loved ones (telling people that God's Sabbath has been changed to Sunday) many will think that they have proof that the oppressive Sunday law is of God, and that they should go along with it to save the economy and the nation!

These lying miracles will fool millions who try to contact dead loved ones who are supposedly communicating from heaven.

To people who do not know the plain word of God, this will be an overwhelming delusion! The Bible forbids anyone to try to contact the dead because when they do, they are inviting evil spirits to speak to them. This is why people who did this type of thing in Bible times were put to death.

The Bible says, Ecclesiastes 9:5. "The dead know not anything." And 1Thess.4:16 teaches that the righteous dead will awake on the very day that Jesus appears in the sky. So do not be fooled by a demon that looks like and sounds so kind and sweet just like a dead loved one! But those in our modern society will fall into this very pit! Already Satan is setting things up for it.

According to the Greeley poll, "One in four Americans has tried to contact the dead! And half of the widows in America and Iceland admit to communication with the dead!" (If they only knew who and what they were talking to they would faint!)

In order to pass a national Sunday law, the constitution must first be affected. The grand principle of separate of church and state must first be undermined (especially the first amendment).

Have you noticed anyone trying to undermine the first amendment lately? In recent years, many states requested a constitutional convention to change it. They came close to getting it! It is alarming that many leaders do not believe the separation of church and state even exists in the constitution! According to Bible prophecy, it will be repudiated. But God expects His children to do all we can to hold it back. The pilgrims shed their blood to provide for us a nation free from religious persecution and intolerance.

Should we see our religious freedom go down the drain and do nothing?

The churches which have Sunday in common will unite in a grand movement so that the world can be converted. Already, religious leaders have been getting their church people into politics. (Since the national Sunday law will be a religious law, it makes sense for the devil to get churches into politics, and try to collapse the separation of church and state to get federal money for religious schools, and get "good" religious laws!) It is shocking, but many political as well as religious leaders are against the separation of church and state now. Have you noticed it? They were not trying to hide it! The Sunday law will be seen as just the thing to solve the horrendous problems we are facing, and to unite the whole Christian world.

Cold chills went down my spine as, in the middle of a Sunday service the preacher with a deep voice that was cold as steel proclaimed that the curse of God rests upon us and will not be removed until the nation repents, and turns back to God by keeping Sunday holy! It will be religious leaders to a large degree who will compel us to "worship the first beast." To worship the first beast, you do not have to join the Catholic Church. All you would have to do is follow the mark of its authority instead of the sign of God's authority and you would be honoring that power more than God; in His sight worshiping it.

Atrocities of the dark ages will be repeated! Society is being manipulated to the degree that in the near future, to receive the "mark of the beast" will be the popular thing to do! Rev.13:3.4-{And I saw one of the heads as if it had been slain, and his fatal wound was healed. And the whole earth was amazed and followed after the beast; and they worshiped the dragon, because he gave his authority to the beast; and they worshiped the beast, saying, "Who is like the beast, and who is able to wage war with him?"}

Those who dare oppose this law will be seen as "reject of society." One of the worst things you can say about a person is to call him a member of a "cult" or a "sect."

Those who oppose the mark of the beast will be seen as "cultists" of the worst kind. They will be worked with by the authorities. When fines and all manner of economic boycott have failed, then they will be sentenced to death. Rev.13:15-17. Men women and children from all walks of life will be fleeing for their lives and hiding in the most desolate areas; or, if caught, cast into jails to await the penalty. War, strife, and terrible calamities of nature will be blamed on them. Like their Savior, and millions of martyrs before them, they will be rejected by loved ones, mocked, and looked upon as the "poor fools who have brought all this trouble on us."

As those loyal to God are brought to court for their faith, the issues about Gods true Sabbath will spread around the world! The truth of God's fourth commandment will be seen in contrast with the counterfeit day which the image of the beast is trying to enforce by law. Notwithstanding the terrorism, pleasure-seeking, and chaos of the world, all will be lead to receive either the "seal of God" or the "mark of the beast."

Spirits of devils go out to deceive the whole world. Rev. 16:13.14. Those who make the word of God their guide will not fall for this world-wide hoax. They will discover the truth about Jesus' holy day, and will observe it is obedience and loving gratitude even in the face of mockery and death.

Then when all have decided (which won't be long), the close of probation comes and Jesus pronounces the most solemn sentence. Rev.22:11-{Let the one who does wrong, still do wrong; and let the one who is filthy, still be filthy; and let the one who is righteous, still practice righteousness; and let the one who is holy, still keep himself holy.}

Every case has been decided for life or death. Then the seven last, terrible plagues of Rev.16 are poured out upon the wicked, and a global conflict takes place under the sixth plague. No matter which way you look at this thing, a great crisis is stealing upon our world. This global conflict will be like nothing you have ever dreamed of before. Your wildest imagination has never pictured it. What will it be like?

THE GLOBAL CONFLICT

SHAKESPEAR Wrote: "There is a line by us unseen that crosses every path, the hidden boundary between God's patience and His wrath."

A great crisis awaits the people of God and even greater crisis awaits the world. Everything that God has created that man has access to is slated for total destruction. If man can destroy it then man will destroy it. The momentous struggle of all the ages is just before us. Daniel 12:1-{Now at that time Michael, the great prince who stands guard over the sons of your people, will arise. And there will be a time of distress such as never occurred since there was a nation until that time; and at that time your people, everyone who is found written in the book, will be rescued.}

When the great warning of Revelation 14:9.10 against receiving the mark of the beast has finished its work, and all have made up their minds, probation closes. God's people have received the great outpouring of the Holy Spirit (the refreshment from the presence of the Lord.) And they are prepared for the trial ahead. They are sealed with the "seal of the Living God." The wicked are finally left to the master they have chosen. They have rejected God's mercy, despised His tender love, and trampled on His law. Now unprotected from Satan's insane wrath, they have no shelter from his power. He will then plunge the entire world into one great final trouble spoken of in Daniel

12. God's wrath poured out on this planet in rebellion will come in the form of seven last plagues brought to view in Revelation 16. Just as the ten plagues of Egypt were against the gods that they worshiped, so the seven last plagues will be especially focused against whose who worship the beast and his image.

As we study this stupendous subject and try to see the whole picture, we find that God is so fair, so kind and to those upon these plagues fall are so disobedient, so hateful, that no one in the entire on-looking universe will accuse God of being unfair for judging this. After the first devastating plagues an angel says Rev. 16:5.6- {And I heard the angel of the waters saying, "Righteous art Thou, who art and who wast, O Holy One, because Thou didst judge these things; for they poured out the blood of saints and prophets, and Thou hast given them blood to drink. They deserve it."}

The heaven defying law has been passed and God's obedient people have been persecuted, mocked, and sentenced to death. And now- Rev.16:1.2-{And I heard a loud voice from the temple, saying to the seven angels, "Go and pour out the seven bowls of the wrath of God into the earth." And the first angel went and poured out his bowl into the earth; and it became a loathsome and malignant sore upon the men who had the mark of the beast and who worshiped the beast.}

Can you imagine sores all over your body?

Notice these gnawing, painful sores will afflict only those who have the mark of the beast and worship his image. What will it be like when this happens?

Can you picture the news telling the shocking story of this gross epidemic? People by the millions who have rejected the "mark" for the purpose of saving their jobs and comforts of life now find that their comfort is gone!

Instead of causing them to repent, and pray to God to forgiveness, these terrible sores only cause them to "blaspheme God" and "gnaw their tongues for pain."

God knows that if He gave them a million years more, they would not change. When the plagues begin to fall, you will know that every case is decided for eternity, and that probation is closed forever. Medical science will be helpless then. Can you picture doctors' offices and drug stores packed with shouting, angry, crying victims? What medicine will relieve the throbbing, biting pain?

Not everyone will get these awful sores. Those who so lately have been persecuted and mocked are now safe. Angels of God protect them. They have loved and been obedient to their Lord even unto death, and now Jesus is very close to them. Though they will be sentenced to death, God's people will not die. Jesus will interpose to save them. While the wicked are perishing with pestilence and famine, God's people are sheltered in the shadow of His hand.

All of a sudden the news breaks the waters have turned to blood! Rev.16:3-{And the second angel poured out his bowl into the sea, and it became blood like that of a dead man; and every living thing in the sea died.} Under the third plague the rivers also turned to blood.

Have you ever seen blood of a dead man? It coagulates into a jelly mass. Those who have hated God's people have tried to shed their blood. Now picture them in pain of their feverish boils turning on their faucets for some relief, and out comes the oozing "blood of a dead man."

Rev.16:7-{And I heard the altar saying, "Yes O Lord God, the Almighty, true and righteous are Thy judgments."}

Look at the beaches! Men are afraid. Where will they drink?

They have tried to shed the blood of the obedient. Now they have blood to drink.

Now something unbelievable happens. The atmospheric layer that shields the earth from scorching heat fails.

Rev.16:8.9-{And the fourth angel poured out his bowl upon the sun; and it was given to it to scorch men with fire. And men were scorched with fierce heat; and they blasphemed the name of God who has the power over these plagues; and they did not repent, so as to give Him glory.}

Horrible pain is now experienced by the wicked. The combination of scorching heat and raw sores is excruciating. Miracles will abound, like Moses' day; some from God, some from Satan. The wicked will not realize that the devil has counterfeited the gifts of the Spirit. Many who have worked miracles and done wonderful works, have trampled on God's Sabbath and persecuted those who honored it. They have felt secure in God's favor. But now their rage is great. Concerning the disobedient, Jesus said in Matt. 7:21-23-{Not everyone who says to Me, 'Lord Lord,' will enter the kingdom of heaven; but he who does the will of My Father who is in heaven. Many will say to Me on that day, 'Lord Lord, did we not prophesy in Your Name and in Your name cast out demons, and in Your name perform miracles?' And then I will declare to them, 'I never knew you; depart from Me, you who practice lawlessness.'} Now their character is revealed. They "blaspheme God and repent not."

Air conditioners will not be able to cope with the intense heat. The buildings will be like ovens. For the wicked, there will be no rest or relief anywhere anytime.

This plague is perfectly suited to the sin of the people. They have honored the "day of the sun" according to the traditions of men and now God gives them sun! The New English Bible says that men were "fearfully burned" during the fourth plague. In that day, many will long for the shelter of God's mercy which they have so long despised.

God's people will still be hiding in desolate places, but He who provided food for Elijah in the wilderness will care for them. While the wicked are dying from the pestilence, angels will shield God's faithful people and supply their wants. God's promise is Isaiah 41:17-{ The afflicted and needy are seeking water, but there is none, And their tongue is parched with thirst; I, the Lord, will answer them Myself, as the God of Israel I will not forsake them.}

While the disobedient is shrieking in pain, reeking with sweat and their parched throats are raw for thirst God's promise to His people is Ps.121:5.6-{The Lord is your keeper; The Lord is your shade on your right hand. The sun will not smite you by day, nor the moon by night.}

In choosing to honor the beast and receive his "mark" instead of honoring God and His "seal." The people have chosen darkness. Now again, God gives them what they have chosen.

Rev.16:10.11-{And the fifth angel poured out his bowl upon the throne of the beast; and his kingdom became darkened; and they gnawed their tongues because of pain, and they blasphemed the God of heaven because of their pains and their sore and they did not repent of their deeds.} Can you imagine that! I think the human mind is inadequate to conceive of the horror that will engulf all society. People of high society; the rich; men of science; and the ignorant masses will be paralyzed with pain, hate, and panic. Society will be in utter chaos!

Of these scourges the Bible says: Joel1:10-12.18-{The field is ruined, the land mourn, for the grain is ruined, The new wine dries up, Fresh oil fails. Be ashamed O farmers, Wail, O vinedressers, for the wheat and the barley; Because the harvest of the field is destroyed. The vine dries up, and the fig tree fails; the pomegranate, the palm also, and the apple tree, all the trees of the field dry up. Indeed, rejoicing dries up from the sons of men. How the beasts groan! The herds of cattle wonder aimlessly because there is no pasture for them; Even the flocks of sheep suffer.}

Oh, if they had only responded to God's great kindness. His arms have been stretched out in love. Now it is too late. The disobedient have decreed that those who have received God's seal cannot buy or sell. Now they themselves are in starving with famine and groping in utter darkness. This supernatural darkness is a fit symbol of the gross darkness that has come upon the minds of those who have turned away from the light of truth.

God's people are still hiding out. They have weeks ago lost their jobs, homes, and fled for their lives before insane men urged on by religious leaders and evil angels They have given up all for Christ. They have seen the wicked perishing while angels of God provided food for them. To the obedient God's promise is given.

Isaiah 33:16-{He will dwell on the heights; His refuge will be the impregnable rock; His bread will be given him; His water will be sure.}

Ps.91:3-10-{For it is He who delivers you from the snare of the trapper, And from the deadly pestilence He will cover you with His pinions. And under His wings you may seek refuge; His faithfulness is a shield and bulwark. You will not be afraid of the terror by night, or of the arrow that flies by day; or of the pestilence that stalks in darkness, or of the destruction that lays waste at noon. A thousand may fall at your side, and ten thousand at your right hand; but it shall not approach you. You will only look on with your eyes, and see the recompense of the wicked, for you have made the Lord, my refuge, Even the Most High, your dwelling place. No evil will befall you, nor will any plague come near your tent.}

By the fifth plague, the wicked world is really angry. They have decided that those who honor God's Sabbath of the Bible are the cause of the horrible convulsions of nature, and they determine to blot them from the earth!

The date is set. When the clock strikes midnight on a certain day, God's obedient people will be sentenced to death! In the midst of the chaos, the sixth angel pours out his vial.

Rev.16:12-14.16-{And the sixth angel poured out is bowl upon the great river, the Euphrates; and its waters was dried up, that the way might be prepared for the kings from the east. And I saw coming out of the mouth of the dragon and out of the mouth of the beast, and out of the mouth of the false prophet, three unclean spirits like frogs; and they gathered them together to the place which in Hebrew is called Har-Magedon.}

Here is where the spirits of devils, by their miracles, prepare the rulers and people of the world, and "gather them together" to fight against God and His people. This is the global conflict. This is the battle of ARMAGEDDON. It is the earth's final battle between good and evil. All have taken sides. The wicked are in the majority and seemly have great advantage. They think they are Goliath and their enemy is small David. But of course this is not the case this time around.

The word "Armageddon" is made of two Hebrew words. "Har" and "Magidon." This is not just a local battle fought in the valley of Megido. The word "Har" means "mountain."

"Armageddon" is the word to denote the great universal battle where the wicked turn against God and His faithful people. This is a world wide battle. The national Sunday law of the U.S. has spread to all the nations of the world. The universal law seeks in one day to strike a decisive blow that will wipe the hated sect from the face of the earth.

When the great Christian coalition of the world comes to the place where it causes (amid miracles and Satanic delusion) the leaders ("kings of the earth") to decree that those who will not go along with the Sunday law should be put to death. It brings the world to the place of sealing its own doom.

The people of God still in prison, some hidden in forests and mountains still plead for God's protection, while companies of armed men hurried by evil angels, are preparing to execute the death sentence. It is now in ever darkest hour, that the God of Israel will interpose to deliver His faithful people.

The date has been set to strike one stunning blow that will wipe the hated sect from the face of the earth. At midnight the death decree goes into effect. At midnight the Mighty God of heaven will interpose to save His people.

Watch what happens next!

Rev.16:17-21-{And the seventh angel poured out his bowl upon the air; and a loud voice came out of the temple from the throne, saying, "It is done." And there were flashes of lightening and sounds and peals of thunder; and there was a great earthquake, such as there had not been since man came to be upon the earth, so great an earthquake was it , and so mighty. And the great city was split into three parts, and the cities of the nations fell. And Babylon the great was remembered before

God, to give her the cup of the wine of His fierce wrath. And every island fled away and the mountains were not found. And huge hailstones about one hundred pounds each, came down from heaven upon men; and men blasphemed God because of the plague of the hail, because its plagues was extremely severe.}

BABYLON THE GREAT THE MOTHER OF ALL

HARLOTS have caused all the nations to drink of the wine of mixture of Christian and sun worshiping practices. Now she drinks of the wine of the wrath of God.

SATAN'S attempt to enforce the death decree against God's humble people is the final climax in his king of swindles. God steps in to save His people. And what a deliverance!

Everything in nature goes haywire. The mountains shake like reed in the wind. The wicked are paralyzed with abject terror and look with amazement upon the situation while the people of God are watching with solemn joy at the great heavenly wonders that are taking place. They instinctively know that the great God Almighty is behind all things and their deliverance is in the midst the chaos. As ragged meteor rocks are hurled to earth in every direction and the sea has unleashed its fury. The whole earth heaves and swells moans and groans. As all life it self is being annihilated. The earths surfaces starts to break apart. The mountain chains have sunk. All of the islands disappear and have seemingly gone into nowhere. The wicked cities of the earth that have become the new Sodom and are swallowed up by tidal waves. The greatest hail storms you can't even imagine are now happening all over the world. This is completely unstoppable. Great hail stones "about the weight of a talent" are wrecking havoc worldwide. A talent is about sixty three pounds. You can imagine that these cannon balls will beat this old earth and the cities of the earth into a pulp.

All these splendid mansions erected by the rich with money embezzled from the poor are dashed into nothing right before their eyes with them in them. Prison walls will tumble down, and Gods people will go free. In fact all will go free. This is all the world chaos.

It is completely impossible to describe the horror and despair of those who have trampled on God's requirements. The enemies of God's law, from ministers down, have a new conception of what truth is. It is too late now. They will now see the true nature of the counterfeit Sabbath that the Roman church has brought in. and the shaky foundation they have been building on. Many will now realize that they are lost and bewildered and confused. But the reality will be undeniable. Reality always wins.

Through this new reality they will be offered the choice to repent. Previously they have chosen the easy and popular way and received the mark of the beast. These things are happening to them because they have followed the religious leaders instead of the plain word of God. They have been led to believe that the majority cannot be wrong. Now they turn on their ministers and bitterly reproach them for their sorry state. Now the ministers have it coming because they too did not heed the plain word of God. So this shows that today's ministers are accepting darkness as a shield in the name of convenience.

WHO ARE YOU GOING TO LISTEN TO?

The global conflict has prepared the wa y for the coming ofChrist and His mighty host of angels which will number in the billions. This will take place during the last of the plagues. Now this is a mighty scene! Watch what happens next!

There appears in the sky a cloud which betokens the coming of the "KING OF KINGS AND THE LORD OF LORDS." In solemn silence God's people gaze upon it as it draws nearer and nearer to this battered earth. Brighter and brighter it appears coming in great clouds of glory. Brighter and brighter in becomes until it is a great white cloud, its glory like a consuming fire. Jesus rides forth as a conqueror riding a white horse. "The armies which were in heaven" were following Him in great glory.

Rev.19:11.14-{And I saw heaven opened; and behold, a white horse, and He who sat upon it is called Faithful and True; and in righteousness He judges and wages war. And the armies which are in heaven, clothed in fine linen, white and clean, were following Him on white horses. So what we have here is a billion angels following The Messiah as he comes to do Battle and CONQUER! All of them are riding white horses. They do not come to earth to lose. They come to slaughter the wicked. The whole heavens seemed filled up with this dazzling scene. Tens of thousands upon tens of thousands of battle ready angels. No pen can describe it. No imagination can imagine it. No one's mind is adequate to imagine the fantastic and holy scene. As the living cloud comes nearer, every eye beholds the bad ass Jesus. This time there is no crown of thorns on his holy brow. There is instead a crown of glory upon His powerful sacred head. His face outshines the dazzling brightness of the sun. Jesus' appearance outshines the sun.

Rev.19:16-{And on His robe and on His thigh He has a name written, "KING OF KINGS AND LORD OF LORDS." As the King of Glory descends on the cloud amid of terrific majesty, and wrapped in flaming fire, the earth trembles. They instinctively know that they are in trouble and they have screwed up. The ground heaves and swells and the very mountains move from their foundations.

Ps.50:3.4-{May our God come and not keep silence; Fire devours before Him, And it is very tempestuous around Him, He summons the heavens above, And the earth, to judge His people:}

Rev.6:15.16-{And the kings of the earth and the great men and the commanders and the rich and the strong and every slave and free man, hid themselves in the caves and among the rocks of the mountains; and they said to the mountains and to the rocks, "Fall on us and hide us from the presence of Him who sits on the throne, and from the wrath of the Lamb.}

The jokes have stopped. Cursing, lying lips are now silent.

In the midst of their terror the wicked hear the voices of God's people joyfully exclaiming:

Isaiah 25:9-{And it will be said on that day, "Behold, this is our God for whom we have waited that He might save us. This is the Lord for whom we have waited; Let us rejoice and be glad in His salvation."}

While the earth is reeling like a drunkard; amid the terrific roar of thunder, and the upheavals of nature, the voice of the Son of God calls His faithful ones of all ages from the grave.

1Thess.4:16.17-{For the Lord Himself will descend from heaven with a shout, with the voice of the archangel, and with the trumpet of God; and the dead in Christ will rise first. Then we who are alive and remain shall be caught up together with them in the clouds to meet the Lord in the air, and thus we shall always be with the Lord.}

God's people are changed: ICor.15:51.52-{Behold, I tell you a mystery; we shall not all sleep, but we shall all be changed, in a moment, in the twinkling of an eye, at the last trumpet; for the trumpet will sound, and the dead will be raised imperishable, and we shall be changed.}

Angels "gather together His elect from the four winds, from one end of heaven to the other." Little children are carried by holy angels to their mother's arms. Friends long separated by death are united, nevermore to part and with songs of gladness ascend together to the city of God. Praise God friend! What a Savior!

I sincerely believe that there is no way for you to read this amazing story and the truths about God' word without having a deep longing to follow Christ all the way and have a part in His glorious kingdom. There will be hard choices either way. I know that you would have never read this unusual book this far unless you had a real interest in learning the truth and following Christ Jesus all the way.

Now that you have learned some of Satan's tactics, and how he has tricked the world into accepting his greatest hoax; you have greater insight on how to escape the trials ahead. And that is by not accepting the mark of the beast; because God has given us His great love and mercy by giving us the warning ages ago.

Now you see the corrupt harlot of Revelation 17, named "Babylon," is the great body of fallen Christianity which has become a mixture of truth and sun-worshiping practices from the ancient Babylon.

You can see that in Revelation 18:4-{And I heard another voice from heaven, saying "Come out of her, my people, that you may not participate in her sins and that you may not receive of her plagues."}

God is calling you today! It is a love call. He has no desire to wipe you out. Consider this your warning. It is God's last call to all born again believers to separate themselves from organizations, no matter how friendly and kind the members are. The ones that are not obeying Jesus command completely and keeping His commandments are under God's judgment.

Very soon, all will have made their choice for the "seal of God" or the "mark of the beast." It is not just a matter of just of two days, it is a matter of worship, of loyalty either to God or to the beast power. Now while Jesus can be found, He is pleading His blood for us in the Most Holy place in heaven. Now when the hour of His judgment is come, and the probation period is forever closed before every case is decided for life and death even now. He is inviting you here and now. Today is the acceptable time of salvation. Choose this day what God you will serve. Jesus Christ is inviting you to surrender all to Him, and have life and peace. Soon it will be too late.

Because the Lovely Jesus Christ shed his precious blood for you and me on the cross of Calvary, I personally choose, by the grace of God to follow Him all the way, to keep His commandments, including His seventh day Sabbath, and receive the "seal of the living God." How about you dear friend? Will you choose to be true to Him too? You will be so happy you did!

Rev.22:14-{Blessed are those who wash their robes, that they may have the right to the tree of life, and may enter by the gates of the city.}

There are other major questions that come to our minds. What about the millennial reign of Christ? After the devil and the wicked are turned to ashes, will the fire of hell go out? (See Ezekiel 28:14-19, Malachi 4:3, Isaiah 47:14).

If the Spirit of God impresses upon you to help get this material to the many precious others that need it desperately, you may contact me and I will be glad to get in touch with them and share these truths with them. You may order one extra as well.

I want to see you in the land of the delight in that wonderful land called heaven, where our lovely Jesus is and where dreams really do come true.

Now may our heavenly father richly bless you and your dear ones as you continue to study His marvelous word! **"The grace of our Lord Jesus Christ be with you all. Amen"**

REVELATION Q&A

(1) Q. What does the word Revelation mean?
A. Unveiling: To reveal or make visible by or as by removing a veil or covering from; disclose. To take off a veil of covering; reveal oneself.

(2) Q. What is the Greek translation of the word "Revelation"?
A. Apokalypsis.

(3) Q. How many times does the word Revelation occur in the New Testament?
A. Eighteen times.

(4) Q. What does the "unveiling" mean?
A. To show or expose to view.

(5) Q. Revelation is the unveiling of who?
A. Jesus Christ.

(6) Q. He (Jesus) made it known by sending who?
A. His angel

(7) Q. The King James Version word for "made known" is what?
A. Signify: To be a sign or indication of; mean. To show or make known, as by a sign, words etc. To have meaning or importance; be significant; matter.

(8) Q. When was the book of Revelation written?
A. In and around the traditionally accepted date of A.D. 95.

(9) Q. Where was it written?
A. It was written on the island of Patmos. Island of the Dodecanese, in the SE Aegean.

(10) Q. Where is Patmos Island?
A. In Asia minor. It is located in the Mediterranean Sea just off the main land of Asia; from the city of Miletus.

(11) Q. Why was John sent to this island?
A. It is where those who were considered "enemies of the state" were incarcerated. He was incarcerated because of the word of God and the testimony of Jesus.

(12) Q. How many books are there in the Bible?
A. There are sixty six books in the Bible.

(13) Q. What does the Scripture mean by the word "blessed?"

A. The word "blessing" in Scripture is similar to the word happy.
(14) **Q.** The book of Revelation is a source of what for those who read it?
A. Blessing. Happiness.
(15) **Q.** In Revelation 1:4 and 1:8. The term who is and who was and who is to come is referring to what?
A. The Holy Trinity or the Triune of God.
(16) **Q.** What is the salutation of Revelation?
A. Grace and peace. They are generated from God, and not man. They are derived from one's relationship with God. He can give grace and peace.
(17) **Q.** Who dispenses out or portions out (make up and give out) peace and grace?
A. The Trinity. All three.
(18) **Q.** Who is the seven spirits before the throne?
A. The seven ministries of the Holy Spirit.
(19) **Q.** Where and who is John instructed to send this Revelation to?
A. The seven churches.
(20) **Q.** What does the term "Tribulation" mean?
A. Suffering from oppression.
(21) **Q.** Who are the seven golden lamp stands?
A. The seven churches of Asia.
(22) **Q.** "and in His right hand He held seven stars." Who are these seven stars?
A. The seven angels of the seven churches.
(23) **Q.** How many successful churches will rise to prominence before Christ's second coming?
A. Seven: The apostolic church, Persecuted church, state church, reformed church, missionary church, apostate church.
(24) **Q.** Christ has ordained who to be the torch bearer in this generation?
A. The church. The church is the salt of the earth. The light of the world.

(25) Q. How many characteristics of Christ was envisioned by John?
A. Ten Characteristics, located in Rev. 1:13-20.
(26) Q. What are the four reasons Christians should not fear?
A. I am the first and last. I am alive forevermore. I am the living one; I was dead. And I hold the keys of death and Hades.
(27) Q. The church of Jesus Christ was founded on what?
A. On the testimony of His personal deity (Matt. 16:18). He said of it: "The gates of Hades will not overcome it."
(28) Q. How many times is it mentioned in the Bible about His coming?
A. Three hundred and eighteen times.
(29) Q. How many rapture passages are there?
A. Twenty six passages.
(30) Q. How many second coming passages?
A. Twenty two passages.
(31) Q. Who is the speaker in Rev. 4:1.2?
A. Jesus Christ is the speaker.
(32) Q. How many heavens are there?
A. Three. The first is the atmospheric heaven. Second is the stellar heaven; known as the universe. The third is the heaven of God.
(33) Q. Where is it suggested God's throne is located?
A. Although the heavens are filled with stars, it seams that behind the North Star there is an empty space. For this reason, it has been suggested that this could be the third heaven. The heaven of God where His throne is.
(34) Q. What is the central object of heaven?
A. The throne of God. It is referred to eight times in Rev. 4:1-6: and eighteen times altogether in chapters 4&5of Rev.
(35) Q. In Rev.4:4- "and around the throne were twenty–four thrones and upon the thrones I saw twenty-four elders sitting, clothed in white garments and golden crowns on their heads." Who are they? Are they angels, spirits, demons or redeemed men?
A. They are redeemed men.

(36) **Q.** In Rev. 4:6 "and before the throne, there was, and is, a sea of glass like crystal." What is the interpretation?
A. A sea in Scripture usually refers to people.
(37) **Q.** In Rev. 4:7, How many creatures are around the throne, and what are they?
A. There are four-living creatures. The first was like a lion. The second was like calf. The third creature had the face like that of a man. The fourth creature was like a flying eagle.
(38) **Q.** In Rev. 1:4 John addresses the seven churches in Asia. "Grace and peace from Him who is and was and who is to come; and from the seven spirits who are before His throne." Who are these seven spirits?
A. The seven ministries of the Holy Spirit. Also in (Isaiah 11:2.)
(39) **Q.** What are the seven ministries of the Holy Spirit?
A. a. The spirit of the Lord.
b. The spirit of wisdom.
c. The spirit of understanding.
d. The spirit of council.
e. The spirit of power.
f. The spirit of knowledge.
g. The spirit of the fear of the Lord.
(40) **Q.** What kind of beings are the living creatures that are in the center and around the throne?
A. Isaiah 6:2 tells us that "Seraphim stood above Him, each having six wings; with two covered his face, and with two he covered his feet, and with two he flew."
(41) **Q.** What is the central role of the four living creatures in heaven? Rev. 4:6.7.
A. It seems they are engaged in the worship of God constantly, but their form suggest that they have other duties to perform. Because of their characteristics, it may well be that they are leaders of the realm they depict. For example, note their forms: The first one is a lion- the leader of the animal kingdom. The second is a calf- the leader of domestic animals. The third is a man- the leader of the angelic hosts. The fourth is a flying eagle- the leader of the kingdom of the fowls of the air.

(42) **Q.** Who is the recipients of Christ's redemption
A. the human race.
(43) **Q.** Rev. 5:1 And I saw in the right hand of Him who sat on the throne a book written inside and on the back, sealed up with seven seals. What is this book?
A. For all intents and purposes the seven sealed scroll (book) is the title deed to the earth. The title deed was given by God to Adam, who lost it through sin to Satan.
(44) **Q.** Rev. 5:2 And I saw a strong angel proclaiming with a loud voice, "Who is worthy to open the book (scroll) and to break its seals?" Who is the only worthy one to open is book?
A. Jesus Christ. Rev 5:5 and one of the elders said to me. "Stop weeping; behold, the Lion that is from the tribe of Judah, the Root of David, has overcome so as to open the book and its seven seals."
(45) **Q.** In Rev. 5:5 It mentions the Lion of the tribe of Judah. What is the interpretations?
A. This is the first of five characteristics described in Rev. 5:5.6. The names of the Lord are never given by accident, but all convey a part of His nature. Since the Lion is king of the beasts and since Judah is the ruling tribe of Israel, this indicates that Christ is to come as King to reign over human affairs.
(46) **Q.** Rev 5:5 mentions the Root of David. What is the interpretation?
A. This is the second of five characteristics mentioned in Rev.5:5. This of course refers to Jesus incarnation or His first birth with His roots in the family of David.
(47) **Q.** Rev. 5:6 Then I saw a lamb, looking as if slain, standing in the center of the throne. Who is around Him?
A. And I saw between the throne (with the four living creatures). "And the elders a lamb standing." This is the third of five characteristics of Rev.5:5.6.
(48) **Q.** Rev.5:6 This is the fifth and sixth characteristics of Christ mentioned. "Having seven horns and seven eyes." What does this mean?

A. Seven horns indicate that the Lamb is not weak. A horn in Scripture indicates power. The eyes speak of judgment of our Lord; including the seven characteristics of the Holy Spirit that rests on Him without measure. Isaiah 11:2 Also John 3:35.

(49) **Q.** Rev.5:8 And when He had taken the book, the four-living creatures and the twenty-four elders fell down before the Lamb, having each one harp, and golden bowls full of incense, What are the golden bowls for?

A. They represent the prayers of the saints. (Holy ones).

(50) **Q.** Who is it that says Christ is worthy to receive these seven things? Power, wealth, wisdom, strength, honor, glory, and blessing.

A. All of the angelic hosts of heaven. Rev. 5:13 And every created thing which is in heaven and on the earth and under the earth and on the sea, and all things in them, I heard saying, "To him who sits on the throne, and to the Lamb, be blessing and honor and glory and dominion forever and ever."

(51) **Q.** Rev.5:5 "And no one in heaven, or on the earth, or under the earth, was able to open the book, or to look into it." Then who is?

A. Jesus Christ is the only one who is qualified. He is the only one who has the title deed.

(52) **Q.** When does the tribulation start, before the seals are opened or after?

A. Before. Rev. 6:1.2 The first seal is broken then the tribulation starts.

(53) **Q.** The seven sealed scroll covers how much time span, of out of the seven years, how long does it take for all the seven seals to come to an end?

A. One fourth of seven years.

(54) **Q.** Breaking or opening the first seal starts off the tribulation. What proceeds it?

A. The rapture.

(55) **Q.** What begins the tribulation period?

A. The actual event that inaugurates the tribulation is found in Daniel 9:27. When the anti-Christ, the "ruler who will come", makes a covenant with Israel for seven years, his signing will trigger the prophet clock of God.

(56) Q. When Christ raptures the church, what must follow next?

A. The anti-Christ will make a covenant with Israel the next day. The next week, or who knows when. There are sufficient signs today to indicate that this event could soon take place.

(57) Q. Who will be in the tribulation?

A. In all probability most of the present generation will go into the tribulation, except the body of Christ.

(58) Q. Once Israel signs the covenant with the anti-Christ, how long is left on earth?

A. Seven years left. From that point God's prophetic clock will begin to tick and humanity will have only seven years left.

(59) Q. In the final analysis, who then, decides whether or not you will go into the tribulation?

A. Your acceptance or rejection of Jesus Christ determines your relation to that time of great misery and heartache.

(60) Q. Can Jesus Christ or anyone stop the tribulation from happening?

A. No, nothing. Daniel 9:26 says, war will continue till the end, and desolation have been decreed.

(61) Q. How many horseman of the apocalypse?

A. In Rev. 6:1-8 There are only four horseman.

(62) Q. Do the sealed judgments, trumpet judgments, and the bowl judgments run concurrently, or chronological?

A. Chronological

(63) Q. Concerning the four horseman of the apocalypse, is it God's intent to show personality through these horsemen on world conditions?

A. World conditions.

(64) Q. What color are the four horsemen?

A. White, red, black and ashen. (sickly pale).

(65) Q. Rev. 6:1.2 {And I saw when the Lord broke one of the seven seals, and I heard one of the four-living creatures saying as with a voice of thunder, "Come." And I looked, and behold, a

white horse, and he who sat on it had a bow; and a crown was given to him; and he went out conquering, and to conquer.} Who is the rider?
A. The anti Christ.
(66) **Q.** What will the anti Christ promise during his tenure?
A. Peace. He promises peace and it will give him control of the world.
(67) **Q.** When will Russia be destroyed?
A. Before the rapture or at the latest will occur at the beginning of the tribulation. See (ezek.39:9).
(68) **Q.** Rev. 6:3.4 {And when He broke the second seal, I heard the second living creature saying, "Come." And another, a red horse, went out, and to him who sat on it, it was granted to take peace from the earth, and that men should slay one another; and a great sword was given to him.} What takes place here?
A. A wide spread world, very bloody war.
(69) **Q.** Some nations will revolt against the anti Christ of taking over the world. Will they be successful in their attempt to throw him off?
A. No
(70) **Q.** The fiery red horse of the apocalypses is a symbol of what?
A. The red horse is obviously a symbol of war. For he has the ability to take peace from the earth and to make men slay each other.
(71) **Q.** Rev. 6:5 {And When He broke the third seal, I heard the third living creature saying, "Come." And I looked, and behold, a black horse; and he who sat on it had a pair of scales in his hand.} What are the scales for?
A. Inflation also tend to grip the world right after a world war. Such will be the case during the tribulation. The balances in the hand of the rider on the black horse indicates a scarcity of food.
(72) **Q.** "And when He broke the third seal, I heard the third living creature saying, 'Come.' And I looked, and behold, a black horse." What is the meaning of the black horse?

A. The black horse is an evident symbol of famine. Black is used to depict famine in other portions of Scripture, and famine often follows war.

(73) **Q.** Rev. 6:6 {And I heard as it were a voice in the center of the four living creatures saying, "A quart of wheat for a denarius, and three quarts of barley for a denarius, and do no harm to the oil and the wine."} What is meant by this?
A. Three measures of barley are about a pint, a minimum barely to sustain ones diet. This then, indicates that a person will have to work for a whole day just to earn enough money to live. The rich however are not so injured. The oil and wine which are traditionally food of the rich.

(74) **Q.** Rev.5:7.8 When the lamb opened the fourth seal, I heard the voice of the fourth living creature saying, "Come." And I looked , and behold, an ashen horse; What does the pale horse represent?
A. The pale horse is literally a livid of corps like, signifying death.

(75) **Q.** Rev. 6:8 And I looked, and behold, an ashen horse; and he who sat on it had the name Death; and Hades was following him. What does this mean?
A. The fact that Death and Hades was following close behind the pale horse of death indicates that these are the unsaved dead. It is also widely believed that these unsaved dead had received the mark of the beast.

(76) **Q.** Rev. 6:8 And I looked, and behold, an ashen horse; and he who sat on it had the name Death; and Hades was following him. And authority was given to them over a fourth of the earth, to kill with sword and with famine and with pestilence and by the wild beasts of the earth. What is meant by "they were given power."
A. The death rate of the first twenty one months of the tribulation period will be tremendously high as a result of war, famine and inflation. In fact, one fourth of all the worlds population will die according to the present world census, that would total about one billion and a half people. The book of

Daniel and Rev. indicates governments as beasts.

(77) Q. What are the four horses-riders of the apocalypses?
A. White horse indicates the anti Christ. The red horse indicates war. The black horse indicates famine, and inflation. The pale horse indicates death for the already unsaved. Those who have already received the mark of the beast.

(78) Q. Rev. 6:9 And when He broke the fifth seal, I saw underneath the alter the souls of those who have been slain because of the word of God, and because of the testimony which they had maintained. Who are these souls?
A. The opening of the fifth seal clearly teaches that after this has begun, there will be a time of great persecution for the children of God. These are tribulation saints. They will be martyred "because of the word of God and the testimony they had maintained.

(79) Q. How many seals of judgment are there?
A. Seven seals of judgment.

(80) Q. What is the death rate of the world during the first twenty one months of the tribulation?
A. About a billion and a half people.

(81) Q. How many horses are of the apocalypse?
A. Four horses

(82).Q. What happens when the sixth seal is opened?
A. A catastrophe on earth. Terror on earth.

(83) Q. What natural disaster could possibly blot out the sun as mentioned in Rev. 6:12?
A. A volcano eruption.

(84) Q. What natural disaster could possibly make the moon look blood red as mentioned in Rev. 6:12?
A. Volcano ash.

(85) Q. Rev. 6:12 and the stars of the sky fell to the earth, as a fig tree casts its unripe figs when shaken by a great wind. What does this mean?
A. This verse indicates that meteors will fall to the ground and hit as hard as unripe figs. (with a thud)

(86) Q. What are the four things that will happen once the anti Christ assumes world wide control?
A. A world war, famine, inflation, and death of twenty five percent of the world population.
(87) Q. During the time the stars fall from the sky as indicated in Rev. 6:13 the people of the earth will be very stubborn, rebellious and God's judgment will be so severe there will be no place on top of the earth to hide. Where will they go?
A. Rev 6:15 And the kings of the earth and the great men and the commanders and the rich and the strong and every slave and free man, hid themselves in the caves and among the rocks of the mountains.
(88) Q. If you were to break down Rev.6 into three different categories, what would you come up with?
A. Judgment by means of natural disasters, war, famine, death of twenty five percent of the world. The prosecution of the saints, and God's supernatural judgment.
(89) Q. In Rev. 6:9 Concerning the martyred saints, What is God's plan here?
A. A great soul harvest is taking place here.
(90) Q. In Rev. 6:8 the pale horse of death with Hades following close behind it. What is shaping here?
A. The grim reaper harvesting of souls for Satan.
(91) Q. In Rev.7- Four angels control the forces of nature. These angels supervise the administration of what two things?
A. They control the wind from the four corners of the earth. They seal the servants of God.
(92) Q. Will there ever be a world wide revival?
A. Absolutely, Yes. During the tribulation Rev.7:9
(93) Q. When will the world's greatest soul harvest take place?
A. During the first twenty one months of the tribulation.
(94) Q. Rev.7:4 The remnants of Israel means the remaining Jews of Israel. Out of those remaining 144,000 will do what?
A. They're will be 144,000 apostle Paul's all over again.
(95) Q. What will be so special about the 144,000 witnesses?
A. They will have the seal of God on their forehead.

(96) **Q.** Why the number 144,000 remnants of Israel?
A. 12,000 people from each of the twelve tribes.
(97) **Q.** Rev. 7:9 After these things I looked, and behold, a great multitude, which no one could count, from every nation and all tribes and peoples and tongues, standing before the throne and before the lamb, clothed in white robes, and palm branches were in their hands. Who are these people?
A. These are the martyred saints of the tribulation.
(99) **Q.** Will the Holy Spirit still be on earth during the tribulation?
A. Yes. There will be countless conversions during this time period. No one can be saved without the Holy Spirit. He will be on earth and with great power.
(100) **Q.** Rev 8:1 and when He broke the seventh seal, there was silence in heaven for how long?
A. For about half an hour. But there will be a silence so ominous that its very nature foreshadows the enormous difficulties that are about to come upon the earth.
(101) **Q.** What do the first five seals reveal?
A. The opening of the first five seals reveals activities on humankind, bringing about great misery on the earth.
(102) **Q.** What does the sixth seal reveal?
A. The opening of the sixth seal seems to be God's reaction against the people for their cruel persecution of His saints.
(103) **Q.** What does the opening of the seventh seal reveal?
A. The opening of the seventh seal introduces the seven trumpets judgments which are all judgments of God sent to earth.
(104) **Q.** Who is the sender and who is the receiver of these trumpet judgments?
A. In the judgments, God is exclusively the sender and the people are the receivers.
(105) **Q.** Who is opening these books?
A. Jesus Christ.
(106) **Q.** The judgments of God are so terrible the angels stand breathless in wonder. Why so severe judgments on mankind?

A. These judgments are the result of generations after generations of rejection of God's redeemer to man, the Lord Jesus Christ.

(107) **Q.** What is God's answer to the prayers of the saints, to avenge their blood?

A. Opening the seventh seal. Rev.8:5 And another angel came and stood at the alter, holding a golden censor; and much incense was given to him, that he might add it to the prayers of all the saints upon the golden alter which was before the throne. And the smoke of the incense, with the prayers of the saints, went up before God out of the angel's hand. And the angel took the censer; and he filled it up with the fire of the altar and threw it to the earth; and there followed peals of thunder and sounds and flashes of lightening and an earthquake.

(108) **Q.** When is it believed that this seventh seal will take place?

A. The breaking of the seventh seal may very well occur at the close of the twenty-first month. At this time it introduces the second quarter or the seven trumpets.

(109) **Q.** How many angels stand before God?

A. Rev.8:2 And I saw seven angels who stand before God; and seven trumpets were given them.

(110) **Q.** What are the seven terrible events that take place at the opening of the sixth seal?

A. a. There was a terrible earthquake.
b. The sun became black as sackcloth.
c. The whole moon became like blood.
d. The stars fell to the earth.
e. The sky was split open apart like a scroll when it was rolled up.
f. Every mountain and island were moved out of their place.
g. and all of mankind hid themselves in caves and among the rocks of the mountains.

(111) **Q.** What are the four things that take place after the opening of the seventh seal?

A. Peals of thunder, and sounds and flashes of lightening, and an earthquake.

(112) **Q.** What judgments follow the sounding of the first trumpet?
A. Rev.8:7-And the first sounded, and there came hail and fire, mixed with blood, and they were thrown to the earth; and a third of the earth was burned up, and all the green grass was burned up.

(113) **Q.** What judgments follow the sounding of the second judgment?
A. Rev.8:8.9-And the second angel sounded, and something like a great mountain burning with fire was thrown into the sea; and a third of the sea became blood: and a third of the creatures, which were in the sea and had life, died; and a third of the ships were destroyed.

(114) **Q.** In Rev. 8:8 mentions a great mountain burning with fire was thrown into the sea. What is this believed possibley to be?
A. The huge mountain is probably a huge meteorite that falls in the Mediterranean Sea. The Mediterranean Sea is the permanent home of the U.S. sixth fleet.

(115) **Q.** What judgments follow the sounding of the third trumpet?
A. Rev.8:10.11-And the third angel sounded, and a great star fell from heaven, burning like a torch, and it fell on a third of the rivers and on the springs of waters; and the name of the star is called wormwood; and many men died from the waters, because they were made bitter.

(116) **Q.** In Rev.8:10-It mentions a great star blazing like a torch fell from the sky. What is this believed to be?
A. The third trumpet introduces us to a burning torch that visibly falls from heaven, indicating it is another meteorite; it must bury itself so deep at just the right spot that it pollutes the water supply of a third of the world's waters.

(117) **Q.** What judgments follow the sounding of the fourth judgment?

A. Rev.8;12-And the fourth angel sounded, and a third of the sun and a third of the moon and a third of the stars were smitten, so that a third of them might be darkened and the day and night might not shine for a third of it, and the night in the same way.
(118) **Q.** What does the trumpet judgments one two and three have in common?
A. They are all judgments by falling meteorites.
(119) **Q.** What happens on the earth as a result of the fourth trumpet judgment?
A. Day and night will seem to be reversed. For there will be sixteen hours of darkness and eight hours of daylight. This judgment is also a prediction of our Lord in Luke 21:25.26.
(120) **Q.** What are the three woes in Rev.8:13? And I looked, and I heard an eagle flying in mid heaven, saying with a loud voice, "Woe, Woe, woe, to those who dwell on the earth, because of the remaining blasts of the trumpet of the three angels who are about to sound!"
A. The three woes of the tribulation period are actually the fifth, sixth, and seventh trumpet judgments.
(121) **Q.** Shaft of the bottomless pit is also known by?
A. The bottomless pit.
(122) **Q.** Where is the bottomless pit believed to be located?
A. The bottomless pit (Abyss) is not hell or Hades. It has been suggested that it may be at the bottom of the great gulf. Fixed in Hades that separates the place of torment and the place of comfort, described as the abode of the dead by Lord Jesus Christ in Luke 16:19-31.
(123) **Q.** Is the fifth trumpet and the first woe synonymous?
A. Yes
(124) **Q.** The three woes of Rev.8:13, and the fifth, sixth, and seventh trumpets. Who are they intended for?
A. Rev.9:4-And they were told that they should not hurt the grass of the earth, nor any green thing, nor any tree, but only the men who do not have the seal of God on their foreheads.
(125) **Q.** Rev.9:2 And he opened the bottomless pit; and smoke went up out of the pit, like the smoke of a great furnace; and the

sun and the air were darkened by the smoke of the pit. Who was let lose?
A. Imprisoned evil spirits in Jude 6 and in Rev.9:11 and they have a king over them, the angel of the Abyss. His name in Hebrew is Abadon (destruction); and in Greek he has the name Apollyon (destroyer).
(126) **Q.** What are the creatures that are let loose from the bottomless pit?
A. Rev.9:3-And out of the smoke came forth locusts upon (into) the earth; and power was given them, as the scorpions of the earth have power.
(127) **Q.** What is the mission of the locust in Rev.9:2?
A. Torment men, but not to kill.
(128) **Q.** What will be mans reaction to the free and evil spirits of Rev.9:3?
A. Rev.9:6- And in those days men will seek death and will not find it; and they will long to die and death flees from them.
(129) **Q.** The freed evil spirits of Rev.9:3 are sent to torment unsaved souls for how long?
A. And they were not permitted to kill anyone, but to torment for five months; and their torment was like the torment of a scorpion when it stings a man.
(130) **Q.** Are believers exempt from the first woe?
A. Yes, Rev. 9:4-And they were told that they should not hurt the grass of the earth, nor any green thing, nor any tree, but only the men that do not have the seal of God on their foreheads.
(131) **Q.** Rev.9:13-15A{And the sixth angel sounded, and I heard a voice from the four horns of the golden altar which is before God, one saying to the sixth angel who had the trumpet, "Release the four angels who are bound at the great river Euphrates." And the four angels, who had been prepared for the hour and day and month and the year were released, so that they might kill a third of mankind.} Are these angels good or bad angels?
A. No! These are evil angels; that is obvious because they are bound. Evidently they are anxious to bring havoc on humans

and the earth but had been bound up to this point.
(132) **Q.** The sixth trumpet judgment is synonymous with the second woe in Rev.9. How many people die in the world?
A. One third of mankind. Rev. 9:15.
(133) **Q.** John hears a voice telling the sixth angel who had the trumpet to release the four angels bound at the Euphrates River. Who is talking to the angel?
A. Doesn't say but It is speculated that the voice is the command of Jesus Christ.
(134) **Q.** What are the three plagues of the sixth trumpet judgment on mankind?
A. Rev.9:18-A third of mankind was killed by these three plagues, by the fire and the smoke and the brimstone, (sulphur) which proceeded out of their mouths.
(135) **Q.** Rev.9;16 {And the number of the armies of the horseman was two hundred million; I heard the number of them.} Are these human armies?
A. No! this is pretty obvious by the description of them that follows. This will be an evil army of two hundred million horse-like creatures with riders on their backs called "horsemen" The four angels bound at the Euphrates seem to be leaders of these evil spirits.
(136) **Q.** What is God's purpose in wiping out so large of the human population in these trumpet judgments?
A. It seams as if the fifth and sixth trumpet judgments is to rid the earth of the incorrigibles in the tribulation who reject the Lord Jesus Christ and salvation through Him. We find that about fifty percent of the world's population will have died. These people cannot possibly populate the millennial kingdom therefore must be purged from the earth.
(137) **Q.** When the fifth trumpet or second woe has come to pass, how many people will have died?
A. About a billion and one half people.
(138) **Q.** How many people will have died during the first half of the tribulation period?
A. Three billion people by today's standards.

(139) **Q.** What are the five major sins that keep man bound to judgment, or propel man to these judgments?
A. a Idolatry, b. murders, c. magic arts, d, sexual immorality, e. thefts.
(140) **Q.** Is God merciful in these judgments?
A. Yes! From the beginning to the end of Rev. Judgments progressively get worse and worse. Once the tribulation starts, people will instinctively know that they are in the judgment period. God is just in his judgments.
(141) **Q.** Rev.10:1-And I saw another angel coming down out of heaven, clothed with a white cloud; and the rainbow was upon his head, and his face was like the sun, and his feet like pillars of fire; Is this Jesus Christ?
A. No! Rev.10:6-The unusual action of the angels lifting his hand toward heaven and swearing by Him who lives forever and ever, who created the heavens, and all that is in them, the earth and all that is in it, and the sea and the things in it, that there shall be no delay no longer.
(142) **Q.** Rev.10:2-and he had in his hand a little book which was open. And he placed his right foot on the sea and his left on the land; what does this indicate?
A. He stands with his right foot in the sea and his left foot on the earth, indicating that he has great authority over all land and sea surfaces.
(143) **Q.** Rev.10:10-And I took the little book out of the angels hand and ate it, and it was in my mouth sweet as honey; and when I had eaten it, my stomach was made bitter. Why was it sweet and why was it bitter?
A. The picture of sweetness in the mouth and bitterness in the belly indicates the typical quality of God's word. The sweetness comes to John in the predictions concerning our blessed Lord's return. The bitterness comes to John in being confronted by the fact that judgment is pronounced on the Earth.
(144) **Q.** Why is the gospel sweet to the taste and bitter in the belly?

A. The gospel is sweet to those who hear and respond, thus being guaranteed eternal salvation as the free gift of God. It is bitter to those who reject it, however, for the same gospel that guarantees salvation to those who receive it, guarantees judgment and damnation to those who reject it.
(145) **Q.** Rev.10:2 The little book in the angels hand that John took and ate of it. What is this little book believed to be?
A. Two possibilities. The first one is believed to be the seven sealed scroll taken from the hand pf God by Christ given to the angel who in turn gives it to John. The second belief is that this little scroll is the new Revelation to John. In either case it is the prophecy of God concerning future events.
(146) **Q.** Rev.10:10 {And I took the little book out of the angels hand and ate it.} Why eat it?
A. The obvious meaning of these symbolic references to "eating the word of God" is that before someone can be a spokes person for God, he must digest the word of God.
(147) **Q.** Rev.10:7-but in the days of the voice of the seventh angel, when he is about to sound, then the mystery of God is finished, as He preached to His servants the prophets. What is this mystery?
A. "The mystery of God" here referred to can only mean salvation. Salvation was made known to God's servant of both old and new testaments. The mystery of salvation is soon coming to a close is apparent by the fact that forty two months of the tribulation period have expired when this statement was given.
(148) **Q.** Rev. 10:11 And they said to me, "You must prophesy again concerning many peoples and nations and tongues and kings." Who is believed to be speaking here?
A. The seven peals of thunder.
(149) **Q.** Rev.10:11 {And they said to men "You must prophesy again concerning many peoples and nations and tongues and kings."} Has this taken place yet?
A. Yes! through the written book of Revelation. This command to the apostle John has been fulfilled. The book of Revelation

has been studied by peoples, nations, languages, and tongues.
(150) **Q.** Where was John when he viewed the mighty angel and the little book?
A. He must have been back on earth after being caught up in the spirit. Rev.10:1 says and I saw another angel coming down out of heaven.
(151) **Q.** What is the second woe?
A. The activities of the two witnesses.
(152) **Q.** Rev.11:8-And their dead bodies will lie in the street of the great city which mystically is called Sodom and Egypt, where also their Lord was crucified. What does Sodom and Egypt mean?
A. Sodom being a symbol of immorality and Egypt being a symbol of materialism.
(153) **Q.** What is the reason or the mission of the two witnesses?
A. To minister and prophesy to the house of Israel.
(154) **Q.** Who is it believed these two witnesses are?
A. Elijah and Moses. Moses represents the first five books. Elijah, the outstanding prophet of Israel, represents the prophetic books. Thus, the two men in Jewish history who must speak of God's dealing with the nation of Israel are Moses and Elijah.
(155) **Q.** Will the temple of God be rebuilt?
A. Yes! Rev.11:1.2-And there was given me a measuring rod like a staff; and someone said, "Rise and measure the temple of God, and the altar, and those who worship in it. And leave out the court which is outside the temple, and do not measure it, for it has been given to the nations; and they will tread under foot the holy city for forty-two months.
(156) **Q.** Where is temple to be built?
A. Where the Dome of the rock sits', a Muslim holy site.
(157) **Q.** The Jewish building of this temple is a symbol of what?
A. The rebuilding of this temple is a rejection of Christ. The fact that Israel will rebuild the temple indicates that she has not received the Messiah.
(158) **Q.** Once it is built who will sit in it?

A. The anti Christ. 2Thess.2:4-who opposes and exalts himself above every so-called god or object of worship, so that he takes his seat in the temple of God, displaying himself as being God.
(159) **Q.** While the two witnesses are on their mission, what power has God given them?
A. Rev.11:6-These have the power to shut up the sky, in order that rain may not fall during the days of prophesying; and they have power over the waters to turn them into blood, and to smite the earth with every plague, as often as they desire.
(160) **Q.** When the two witnesses are done with their testimony, who will slay them?
A. Rev.11:7-And when they have finished their testimony, the beast that comes up out of the abyss will make war with them, and overcome and kill them.
(161) **Q.** The two witnesses will be slain and will lie in the streets for how long?
A. Rev.11:11-And after the three and a half days the breath of life from God came into them, and they stood on their feet; and great fear fell upon those who were beholding them.
(162) **Q.** What became of the two witnesses after the breath of life from God set them on their feet again?
A. And they heard a loud voice from heaven saying to them, "Come up here." And they went up into heaven in the cloud, and their enemies beheld them.
(163) **Q.** Once the two witnesses were raptured, what happened in the city of Jerusalem?
A. Rev.11:13-And in that hour there was a great earth quake, and a tenth of the city fell; and seven thousand people were killed in the earthquake, and the rest were terrified and gave glory to the God of heaven.
(164) **Q.** What is the second woe?
A. The two witnesses of Rev.11
(165) **Q.** What is the third woe in Rev.13?
A. The seventh trumpet.
(166) **Q.** Does the seventh trumpet initiate a response on earth?

A. No! The blowing of the seventh trumpet does not initiate anything on earth. Instead, it merely introduces the next set of judgments. The seven bowls occurring exclusively on earth.

(167) **Q.** What are the two principle forms Satan has used to deceive human beings?

A. Religion and government.

(168) **Q.** Rev.12 is what part of the tribulation?

A. Rev.12 introduces the second half of the tribulation period by giving a heavenly recap of the great conflict of the ages, bringing us up to date.

(169) **Q.** Governments have been the main cause of death to humanity on earth. Just during the twentieth century, approximately how many people have been killed?

A. Instead of doing good, governments have been the principle cause of much suffering to the present day. During the twentieth century, more than 160-180 million people have been murdered, starved, or imprisoned by governments.

(170) **Q.** Rev.12:1.2-And a great sign appeared in heaven: a woman clothed with the sun, and the moon under her feet, and on her head a crown of twelve stars; and she was with child; and she cries out, being in labor and in pain to give birth. What does this passage mean?

A. The child is none other than Jesus Christ our Lord. The fact that this woman is seen clothed with the sun, with the moon under her feet is most illuminating. These objects are light conveying objects. The moon is a reflector, the sun a source of light. They are symbolic of Israel as God's light bearer to humankind. The twelve stars are the twelve tribes of Israel.

(171) **Q.** What does the term "a great red dragon" mean?

A. He is red because he is the motivating force behind much of the blood shed in human history, from Cain to present.

(172) **Q.** What does the term "that ancient serpent" mean?

A. "That ancient serpent" refers to the first time the devil is seen in the Bible in the Garden of Eden.

(173) **Q.** What does the term "the devil" mean in Rev.12:9?

A. "The devil" is the term used in the gospels for the enemy of God. It means "slanderer or accuser."
(174) **Q.** What does the term "Satan" mean in Rev.12:9?
A. Satan means "adversary." The devil is the adversary of God's children.
(175) **Q.** What does the term "the accuser of our brethren" mean in Rev. 12:10?
A. "The accuser of our brothers" indicates Satan's work before the throne of God today, seeking to discredit the saints before God.
(176) **Q.** Rev 12:3 {And another sign appeared in heaven: and behold, a great red dragon having seven heads and ten horns, and on his heads were seven diadems.} Who is this and what does it mean?
A. This is Satan and his evil government. The seven crowned heads probably refer to the seven stages of the Roman Empire. In fact the Roman government is in its sixth stage now. The ten horns refer to the ten kings who will be dominant during the tribulation. From whom the anti-Christ (the seven head) will receive his power.
(177) **Q.** Rev.12:4 {And his tail swept away the third of the stars of heaven, and threw them to the earth. And the dragon stood before the woman who was about to give birth, so that when she gave birth he might devour her child.} What does this mean?
A. This probably refers to the fall of Satan described in Isaiah 14 and his attitude. Satan initiated what Bible scholars called "the conflict of the ages" attempting to stamp out all the seed of the woman.
(178) **Q.** Rev.12:5-And she gave birth to a son, a male child, who was to rule all the nations with a rod of iron; and her child was caught up to God and to His throne. Who is this child?
A. This is without a doubt Jesus Christ our Lord and Savior.
(179) **Q.** Rev.12:6-And the woman fled into the wilderness where she had a place prepared by God, so that there she might be nourished for one thousand two hundred and sixty days. Who is this woman?

A. Daniel 11:40-45 speaks of a war during the middle of the tribulation, which will affect all of the countries of the world. Israel will flee into the wilderness during the last half of the tribulation period. God will feed her, and supply her every need for three and one half years.

(180) **Q.** Rev. 12:9 {And the great dragon was thrown down, the serpent of old who is called the devil, and Satan, who deceives the whole world; he was thrown down to the earth, and his angels were thrown down with him.} When does this take place?

A. In the middle of the tribulation period the conflicts between the holy and the unholy will reach a climax. Satan and his host will be banished from heaven and be cast to earth. He now will be filled with great fury.

(181) **Q.** Rev.12:10 {And I heard a loud voice in heaven, saying, "Now the salvation, and the power, and the kingdom of our God and the authority of His Christ have come, for the accuser of our brethren has been thrown down, who accuses them before our God day and night.} What does this mean?

A. The great conflict of the ages is coming to a close. The time has finally come for the heavenly host to exert its authority over the unholy. The beginning of Christ's rule starts here for eternity.

(182) **Q.** Rev.12:12 {"For this reason, rejoice, O heavens and you who dwell in them. Woe to the earth and the sea, because the devil has come down to you, having great wrath, knowing that he has only a short time."} How long does he have?

A. Knowing he has but a short time like only three and one half years. He will be filled with wrath and hatred.

(183).**Q.** Rev. 12:13 {And when the dragon saw that he was thrown down to the earth, he persecuted the woman who gave birth to the male child.} Who is this woman?

A. Although heaven will rejoice because Satan is out, earth will not share this rejoicing, for Satan will take command of the earth and its operations against his greatest enemy, the nation of Israel.

(184) Q. Rev.12:14 {And the two wings of the great eagle were given to the woman, in order that she might fly into the wilderness to her place, where she was nourished for a time and times and a half of time, from the presence (face) of the serpent.} What does this mean?
A. The remnants of Israel will flee their home land to the desert mountain's where a place has been prepared for them and they will live for three and one half years of the second half of the tribulation.
(185) Q. Rev.12:15 {And the serpent poured water like a river out of his mouth after the woman, so that he might cause her to be swept away with the flood.} What does this mean?
A. There are four possible reasons why this happens.
a. Satan will actually divert rivers and bodies of water into the desert where Israel is being kept by God.
b. He will attempt to flood her with false teachings.
c. Satan will send an army after them.
e. Torrential rains in the region.
(186) Q. Rev.12:17 {And the dragon was enraged with the woman, and went off to make war with the rest of her offspring, who keep the commandments of God and hold to the testimony of Jesus.} What does this mean?
A. Satan's attempt to exterminate the Jews in the desert will be thwarted supernaturally. He will then go after the Jews who have recognized Jesus as their Messiah.
(187) Q. What would have happened to the world if Israel would have accepted Jesus two thousand tears ago?
A. It would have altered history dramatically.
(188) Q. Why has God unleashed Satan to go after the Jews?
A. To get them to accept Jesus Christ as their Messiah.
(189) Q. What has been the price the Jews paid for not accepting Jesus as the Messiah?
A. The world wants to exterminate them. They are hated worldwide. This is God's judgment for disobedience.
(190) Q. What is the nationality of the anti-Christ.
A. The Bible teaches that he will be a Roman-Grecian-Jew.

(191) Q. How will the anti-Christ come to power?
A. He will assume power by the strength of diplomacy.
(192) Q. The one world government is predicted in the image of Nebuchadnezzar in Daniel 2. Through what organization will the anti-Christ bring forth his one world government?
A. The United Nations.
(193) Q. How will the anti-Christ dominate the world economy?
A. Such an economy has been suggested in the European Common Market.
(194) Q. How will the anti-Christ gain control of religion?
A. Through the world council of churches.
(195) Q. In Rev.17 the harlot is who?
A. The Ecumenical church (from the inhabited world).
(196) Q. The anti-Christ will sign a covenant with Israel for seven years. How long before it is broken?
A. Three and one half years.
(197) Q. Will the anti-Christ give Israel peace?
A. Yes! Then no! For the first three and a half years only then he will seek to distort her. He will double cross her.
(198) Q. Will the anti-Christ be killed?
A. Yes! Rev.17:8-The beast that you saw was and is not, and is about to come up out of the abyss and go to destruction. And those who dwell on the earth will wonder, whose name has not been written in the book of life from the foundation of the world, when they see the beast, that he was and is not and will come.
(199) Q. When will the anti-Christ die?
A. The anti-Christ will die in the middle of the tribulation.
(200) Q. Will the anti-Christ be resurrected?
A. Yes! Rev.17:8- says he will come up out of the abyss. Satan will indwell this body.
(201) Q. Will the anti-Christ be destroyed the second time?
A. Yes! By Christ Himself at His second coming Rev.19:11-20- And I saw heaven opened; and behold, a white horse, and He who sat upon it is called faithful and true; and in righteousness He judges and wages war. And His eyes are a flame of fire, and

upon His head are many diadems; and He has a name written upon Him which no one knows except Himself. And He is clothed with a robe dipped in blood; and His name is called the Word of God. And the armies which are in heaven, clothed in fine lined, white and clean, were following him on white horses. And from His mouth comes a sharp sword, so that with it He may smite the nations; and He will rule them with a rod of iron; and He treads the wine press of the fierce wrath of God, the Almighty. And on His robe and on His thigh He has a name written, "KINGS OF KINGS AND LORD OF LORDS." And I saw an angel standing in the sun; and he cried out with a loud voice, saying to all the birds which fly in mid-heaven, "Come. Assemble for the great supper of God;in order that you may eat the flesh of kings and the flesh of commanders and the flesh of might men and the flesh of horses and of those who sit on them and the flesh of all men, both free and slaves, and small and great." And I saw the beast and the kings of the earth and their armies, assembled to make war against Him who sat upon the horse, and against His army. And the beast was seized, and with him the false prophet, who performed the signs in his presence, by which he deceived those who had received the mark of the beast and those who worshiped his image; these were thrown alive into the lake of fire which burns with brimstone.

(202) **Q.** The anti-Christ will be fatally wounded and die during the tribulation. How will he come back to life?
A. Satan will duplicate The death, and the resurrection of Jesus Christ. The anti-Christ will be resurrected and the body indwelt by Satan himself. Rev. 13:3-And I saw one of its heads as if it had been slain (smitten to death) and his fatal wound was healed. And the whole world was amazed and followed after the beast.

(203) **Q.** Will people worship Satan in the last days?
A. Yes! Many people will follow him and worship him. Rev. 13:4-and they worshiped the dragon, because he gave his authority to the beast; and they worshiped the beast, "who is like the beast, and who is able to wage war with him?"

(204) **Q.** When Satan resurrects the anti-Christ, what things will he have to say and do?
A. Rev.13:6.7- And he opened him mouth in blasphemes against God, to blaspheme His name and His tabernacle, that is, those who dwell in heaven. And it was given to him to make war with the saints and to overcome them; and authority over every tribe and people and tongue and nation was given to him.
(205) **Q.** Who on earth will worship the anti-Christ during the tribulation?
A. Rev.13:8-And all who dwell on earth will worship him, everyone whose name has not been written from the foundation of the world in the book of life of the lamb who has been slain.
(206) **Q.** Rev.13:11 {And I saw another beast coming up out of the earth; and he had two horns like a lamb, and he spoke as a dragon.} Who is this?
A. This is the false prophet.
(207) **Q.** What will be the false prophet's main function or job?
A. Rev.13:12-And he exercises all the authority of the first beast in his presence. And he makes the earth and those who dwell in it to worship the first beast, whose fatal wound was healed.
(208) **Q.** Why is a false prophet necessary?
A. Since humanity is incurably religious, a world dictator must provide people an outlet for their religious inclinations.
(209) **Q.** Will the false prophet be religious?
A. Yes! Rev.13:12-And he exercises all the authority of the first beast in his presence. And he makes the earth and those who dwell in it to worship the first beast, whose fatal wound was healed.
(210) **Q.** What nationality will the false prophet be of?
A. "Then I saw coming out of the earth." Many Bible teachers suggest that his coming out of the earth indicates that he will not come out of the sea of peoples, as the first beast does. That is, he will not be of mixed nationality; that he comes out of the earth (around Palestine). Many people believe he will be a Jew.
(211) **Q.** What is the satanic trinity?
A. The anti-Christ, anti-Christ resurrected, and the false prophet.

(212) **Q.** What power will the false prophet have?
A. Rev.13:12-And he exercises all the authority of the first beast in his presence. And he makes the earth and those who dwell in it to worship the first beast, whose fatal wound was healed.
(213) **Q.** How does the mark of the beast come about?
A. It is an order issued by the false prophet. Rev.13:15-And there was given to him to give breath to the image of the beast, that the image of the beast might even speak and cause as many as do not worship the image of the beast to be killed.
(214) **Q.** What is the mark of the beast?
A. Rev.13:18-Here is wisdom. Let him who has understanding calculate the number of the beast, for the number is that of a man; and his number is six hundred and sixty six.
(215) **Q.** When will the false prophet come about?
A. In the second half of the tribulation.
(216) **Q.** The false prophet will create an image of the beast. What is significant about this image or unusual about it?
A. Rev.13:15-And there was given to him to give breath to the image of the beast, that the image of the beast might even speak and cause as many as do not worship the image of the beast to be killed.
(217) **Q.** Where will the mark of the beast be put on your body?
A. Rev.13:16-And he causes all, the small and the great, and the rich and the poor, and the free men and the slaves, to be given a mark on their right hand, or on their forehead.
(218) **Q.** Who will be given the mark of the beast?
A. Rev.13:16- Everybody! The great and the small, the rich and the poor and the free and the slave.
(219) **Q.** What will happen to those who will not take the mark of the beast?
A. They will be beheaded. Rev.20:4-And I saw thrones, and they sat upon them, and judgment was given to them. And I saw souls of those who had been beheaded because of the testimony of Jesus and because of the Word of God, and those who had not worshiped the beast or his image, and had not received the mark upon their forehead and upon their hand; and they came to life

and reigned with Christ for a thousand years.

(220) **Q.** What method will the false prophet use?
A. It is widely believed the guillotine will be used.

(221) **Q.** Rev.14:1 {And I looked, and behold, the lamb was standing on Mount Zion, and with Him one hundred and forty four thousand having His name and the name of His Father written on their foreheads.} Where is this taking place?
A. This chapter introduces a scene in heaven.

(222) **Q.** In Rev.14:1 {And I looked, and behold, the lamb was standing on Mount Zion, and with Him one hundred and forty four thousand having His name and the name of His Father written on their foreheads.} When is this taking place?
A. Mid tribulation, just before the seventh trumpet.

(223) **Q.** Rev.14:1 {And I looked, and behold, the lamb was standing on Mount Zion, and with Him one hundred and forty four thousand having His name and the name of His Father written on their foreheads.} Who are these people?
A. Without being dogmatic, it is tenderly believed that the one hundred and forty four thousand in chapter 14 are probably the most outstanding saints of the church from the early days of the spread of the gospel to the rapture of the church.

(224) **Q.** In Rev.14:6,8,9,15-18.There are five special angels from heaven giving warnings. Why are they commissioned for this job?
A. First of all, it is astounding that an angel is commissioned to go forth preaching the everlasting gospel. This is a human's job. This astounding state of affairs can only be an indication of the severity of the circumstances on earth during this time. One of the God's faithful practices in all judgments has been to send adequate warning prior to judgment. The seven bowls of judgment is about to be poured out.

(225) **Q.** The great persecution of the tribulation saints referred to in the fifth seal of chapter six prior to the middle of the tribulation is protected by who?

A. Persecutions and beheadings will be done under the auspices (patronage and protection) of the Ecumenical church (National Council of churches).

(226) **Q.** Before God pours judgment on the earth what does he do in Rev.14? In what way does God send His last warning?
A. He sends five warning angels to earth to tell mankind to either fear God and serve Him or burn in hell for all eternity.

(227) **Q.** What is the warning of the five angels in Rev. 14
A. To preach the everlasting gospel. To warn about the mark of the beast.

(228) **Q.** What happens to the one who takes the mark of the beast on his hand or forehead?
A. Rev.14:9.10-And another angel, a third one followed them, saying with a loud voice, if anyone worships the beast and his image, and receives a mark on his forehead or upon his hand, he also will drink of the wine of the wrath of God, which is mixed in full strength in the cup of His anger; and he will be tormented with fire and brimstone in the presence of the holy angels and in the presence of the lamb.

(229) **Q.** Will there be a second chance for those who receive the mark of the beast?
A. Absolutely not! Rev.14;11- "And the smoke of their torment goes up forever and ever; and they have no rest day and night, those who worship the beast and his image, and whoever receives the mark of his name.

(230) **Q.** What happens to the ones who remains faithful to Jesus and obeys God's commandments unto death?
A. Rev. 14:13- And I heard a voice from heaven, saying, "Write, 'Blessed are the dead who die in the Lord from now on!" "Yes," says the Spirit, "that they may rest from their labors, for their deeds follow them."

(231) **Q.** Rev.14:14 {And I looked, and behold, a white cloud, and sitting on the cloud was one like a son of man, having a golden crown on His head, and sharp sickle in His hand. This is referred to as the reapers.} When does this take place?

A. It is a prediction of the battle of the great day of God Almighty. It is a prophetic fore glimpse of what is to come when Christ destroys the anti-Christ and his followers.

(232) **Q.** Rev.15:1 {And I saw another sign in heaven, great and marvelous, seven angels who had seven plagues, which are the last, because in them the wrath of God is finished.} What is happening here?

A. The seven angels and the seven plagues are the seven bowl judgments. These are the last judgments of God to humankind.

(233) **Q.** Rev.15:2 {And I saw as it were, a sea of glass mixed with fire, and those who had come off victorious from the beast and from his image and from the number of his name, standing on the sea of glass, holding harps of God.} Who are these people?

A. These are martyred tribulation saints who overcame the beast by not worshiping his image. A sea of glass indicates a multitude no one can count. Mixed with fire indicates their trial on earth. Holding harps suggest they are now content and happy.

(234) **Q.** What is the eternal reward for a martyred saint?

A. In Rev.2:10-'Do not fear what you are about to suffer. Behold, the devil is about to cast some of you in prison, that you may be tested, and you will have tribulation ten days. Be faithful until death, and I will give you the crown of life.

(235) **Q.** Rev.15:5{After these things, I looked, and the temple of the tabernacle of testimony in heaven was opened.} What is this?

A. The testimony that emanates from the tabernacle is seen in the Ark of the Covenant. God has a covenant with Israel and with every member of the church of Christ.

(236) **Q.** Rev.15:8 {And the temple was filled with smoke from the glory of God and from His power; and no one was able to enter the temple until the seven plagues of the seven angels were finished.} Why wasn't anybody permitted in this temple?

A. In other words, from the middle of the tribulation period, no created being will have access to the presence of God on His throne until the end of the tribulation. For He will not be dealing with people in mercy, as is His usual custom. During the latter three and one half years of the tribulation, He will be dealing with human beings in judgment.

(237) **Q.** What is the purpose of bringing about the great tribulation?

A. The first is to bring souls to Him. Then destroy the followers of the anti-Christ. Then to brings Jews to recognize Jesus as the Messiah. In the mean time shake up mankind out of their ordinary sense of security and make them look to Him.

(238) **Q.** When does the seven bowl judgments occur?

A. When the seven bowl judgments start, it signifies the second half of the tribulation.

(239) **Q.** In Matt. 24:21-Jesus referred to as "the great distress in those days." What was He meaning?

A. He was talking about the seven bowl judgments.

(240) **Q.** How long will the seven bowl judgments last?

A. The entire second half of the tribulation, which is three and one half years.

(241) **Q.** Who is the recipient of the first five bowls?

A. Worshipers of the beast. Only those containing the mark of the beast.

(242) **Q.** What is the first bowl judgment?

A. Rev.16:2-And the first angel went and poured out his first bowl into the earth; and if became a loathsome and malignant sore upon the men who had the mark of the beast, and who worshiped his image.

(243) **Q.** What is the second bowl judgment?

A. Rev.16:3-And the second angel poured out his bowl into the sea, and it became blood like that of a dead man; and every living thing in the sea died.

(244) **Q.** What is the third bowl judgment?

A. Rev.16:4-And the third angel poured out his bowl into the rivers and the springs of waters; and they became blood.

(245) **Q.** What is God's reasoning for these blood bowls?

A. Rev;16:5-And I heard the angel of the waters saying, "Righteous art Thou, who art and who wast, O Holy One, because Thou didst judge these things; For they poured out the blood of the saints and prophets, and Thou hast given them blood to drink. They deserve it."

(246) **Q.** What is the fourth bowl judgment?
A. And the fourth angel poured out his bowl upon the sun; and it was given to it to scorch men with fire.

(247) **Q.** What was the response from mankind from the forth bowl judgment?
A. Rev.16:9-And the men were scorched with fierce heat; and they blasphemed the name of God who has the power over these plagues; and they did not repent, so as to give Him glory.

(248) **Q.** What is the fifth bowl judgment?
A. Rev.16:10-And the fifth angel poured out his bowl upon the throne of the beast; and his kingdom became darkened; and they gnawed their tongues because of pain.

(249) **Q.** What is the response from the kingdom of the beast as a result of the fifth bowl judgment?
A. Rev.16:11-and they blasphemed the God of heaven because of their pains and their sores; and they did not repent of their deeds.

(250) **Q.** What is the sixth bowl judgment?
A. Rev.16:12-And the sixth angel poured out his bowl upon the great river, Euphrates; and its waters was dried up, that the way might be prepared for the kings from the east.

(251) **Q.** How do the armies end up in the valley of Megiddo?
A. Rev. 16:13.14-And I saw coming out of the mouth of the dragon and out of the mouth of the beast and out of the mouth of the false prophet, three unclean spirits like frogs; for they are spirits of demons, performing signs, which go out to the kings of the whole world, to gather them together for the war of the great day of God, the Almighty.

(252) **Q.** What is the seventh bowl judgment?
A. Rev.16.:17-21-And the seventh angel poured out his bowl upon the air; and a loud voice came out of the temple from the

throne, saying, "It is done" And there were flashes of lightening and sounds and peals of thunder; and there was a great earthquake, such as there had not been since man came upon the earth, so great an earthquake was it, and so mighty. And the great city was split into three parts, and the cities of the nations fell. And Babylon the great was remembered before God, to give her the cup of the wine of His fierce wrath. And every island fled away, and the mountains were not found. And huge hailstones, about one hundred pounds each, came down from heaven upon men; and men blasphemed God because of the plague of the hail, because its plagues were extremely severe.

(253) **Q.** Where is the Megiddo Valley located for the armies of the world to gather?
A. The Megiddo Valley is located close to the center of Palestine.

(254) **Q.** Where on earth is the Megiddo Valley?
A. It is in Israel. Its precise location is between southwest of the Golan Heights and just north of the west bank. Just east of the Mediterranean Sea in North Israel.

(255) **Q.** What does Easter mean?
A. Easter is not a Christian name. It means "Ishtar" one of the titles of the Babylon queen of heaven, whose worship by the children of Israel was such an abomination in the sight of God.

(256) **Q.** Who is the harlot in Rev.17?
A. the harlot is the government and the religious system of Babylon.

(257) **Q.** Where is the harlot located?
A. It originated in Babylon. Her destruction will be in Babylon.

(258) **Q.** What will be the religion of Babylon?
A. Babylon is where the Catholic faith originated. Babylon is where it will meet its destruction.

(259) **Q.** Why is Babylon of great importance?
A. Babylon is considered Satan's stronghold and headquarters until it was relocated to Rome.

(260) **Q.** Why does Rev.17:5 refer to Babylon as a mystery, the great. The mother of harlots and of the abominations of the earth?
A. The Catholic faith was born from darkness, in secret. A plan by Satan to bring about a deliverer. A child was conceived miraculously. The child was worshiped by all even Israel. It all started as a cult. This is why to this day Catholics still reject Christ in personal faith.
(261) **Q.** Has the Catholics been an abomination to the whole earth?
A. Yes! Catholics have been known to slaughter hundreds of thousands of the faith in Jesus Christ.
(262) **Q.** Will the Catholics persecute Christians again?
A. Yes! The religionist will ride on the back of the beast. The beast will carry her for a while. Then the beast will get tired or her. The beast will use her then abuse her. Then the beast will throw her ass to the ground. Why? "because she is a harlot."
(263) **Q.** What will happen when the beast gets tired of her?
A. Rev.17:16-And the ten horns which you saw, and the beast, these will hate the harlot and will make her desolate and naked, and will eat her flesh and will burn her up with fire.
(264) **Q.** So what is God essentially doing here in Rev.17?
A. Since Satan is the author of this religious system and Satan will occupy the body himself of the resurrected anti-Christ. He will himself destroy this religion. Rape it, kill it, and then burn it to the ground.
(265) **Q.** How does this fit into God's plan?
A. Rev.17:17-"For God has put it in their hearts to execute His purpose by having a common purpose, and by giving their kingdom to the beast, until the words of God should be fulfilled.
(266) **Q.** What clue do we have about the connection between the harlot and the Catholic religion?
A. Rev.17:4-And the woman was clothed in purple and scarlet, and adorned with gold and precious stones and pearls, and having in her hand a gold cup full of abominations and of the unclean things of her immorality,

(267) **Q.** When the religious system of Babylon is destroyed, what will the people of the earth worship next?
A. The beast. Once the religious system is done away with, this clears the way for the anti-Christ to fulfill his long time dream of Satan to get people to worship him.
(268) **Q.** When will she be destroyed?
A. The religious system will be destroyed in the middle of the tribulation.
(269) **Q.** Who will destroy the religious system of Babylon?
A. The resurrected anti-Christ along with the ten kings with him.
(270) **Q.** When will the Babylon fall, and the governmental system with it?
A. At the end of the tribulation.
(271) **Q.** Why does God want to destroy Babylon the great?
A. Rev.18:24-And in her was found the blood of prophets and of saints and of all who have been slain on the earth.
(272) **Q.** Why is Babylon cursed?
A. Rev.18:2-And he cried with a mighty voice, saying, "Fallen, fallen is Babylon the great! And she has become a dwelling place to demons and a prison of every unclean spirit, and a prison of every unclean and hateful bird.
(273) **Q.** If the destruction will be swift, then how long will it take to destroy Babylon the great?
A. For in one hour such great wealth has been laid waste!' And every shipmaster and every passenger and sailor, and as many as make a living by the sea, stood at a distance.
(274) **Q.** Sudden destruction will come upon Babylon, how will she be destroyed?
A. Rev.18:8- "For this reason in one day her plagues will come, pestilence and mourning and famine, and she will be burned up with fire; for the Lord God who judges her is strong.
(275) **Q.** What is the response on earth from her destruction?
A. Rev.18:9-"And the kings of the earth, who committed acts of immorality and lived sensuously with her, will weep and lament over her when they see the smoke of her burning.

(276) **Q.** What will be the response in heaven over the destruction of Babylon the great?
A. Rev.18:20-"Rejoice over her ,O heaven, and you saints and apostles and prophets, because God has pronounced judgment for you against her."
(277) **Q.** Will Babylon ever recover?
A. Absolutely not! Rev.18:21-24- And a strong angel took up a millstone like a great millstone and threw it into the sea, saying. "Thus will Babylon, the great city, be thrown down with violence, and will not be found any longer. And the sound of the harpist and musicians and flute-players and trumpeters will not be heard in you any longer; and no craftsman of any craft will be found in you any longer; and the sound of a mill will not be heard in you any longer; and the light of a lamp will not shine in you any longer; and the voice of the bridegroom and bride will not be heard in you any longer; for your merchants were the great men of the earth, because all the nations were deceived by your sorcery. And in her was found the blood of the prophets and of saints and of all who have been slain on the earth."
(278) **Q.** Who is the bride groom?
A. Christ is the bridegroom at the marriage of the lamb.
(279) **Q.** Who is the bride?
A. The church is the bride.
(280) **Q.** When will the marriage take place?
A. By the time the tribulation on the earth has come to a close, the marriage of the Lamb must have taken place.
(281) **Q.** Where will the marriage of the Lamb take place?
A. Marriage of the Lamb will take place in heaven.
(282) **Q.** Who are the guests of the bride?
A. All of the believing dead from Adam until the resurrection of Christ will be guests at this feast.
(283) **Q.** Where does the honey moon take place?
A. After the marriage of the Lamb Christ brings His bride to earth to reign with Him for one thousand years. There will be one thousand years of peace.

(284) **Q.** How does the believer know where he stands on the one thousands year reign of Christ?
A. Rev.14:13-And I heard a voice from heaven, saying, "Write, 'Blessed are the dead who die in the Lord from now on!" "Yes," says the Spirit, "that they may rest from their labors, for their deeds follow with them." Whatever you actions were on earth will follow you into eternity.
(285) **Q.** What will happen on earth when Christ returns?
A. It will be a day of vengeance. He will smite the nations, destroy His enemies. He will also seize the beast and the false prophet. He will establish His kingdom and reign on earth. See Rev.19:11-21.
(286) **Q.** When will Christ come?
A. At the end of the tribulation.
(287) **Q.** What will be the signs of His coming?
A. After the bowl judgments, all of heaven will rejoice. Matt. 24:27.28-Jesus said, "For just as the lightening comes from the east, and flashes even to the west, so shall the coming of the Son of Man be." Wherever the corps is, there the vultures will gather.
(288) **Q.** Rev.19:14- And the armies which were in heaven, clothed in fine linen, white and clean, were following Him on white horses. Who are these armies?
A. The armies of heaven consist of the angelic host, the Old Testament saints, the church and the tribulation saints.
(289) **Q.** When Christ comes, He will wage war. People will die. What will happen to their bodies?
A. Rev.19:21-And the rest were killed with the sword which came from the mouth of Him who sat upon the horse, and all the birds were filled with their flesh.
(290) **Q.** What does a sharp two-edged sword mean?
A. The sharp sword here has lead some to believe that is the sword of the spirit, which is the word of God. The word for sword indicates a long Thracian sword, or one which is unusually large or longer than most swords. The same word is sometimes used to describe a javelin. A sword sufficiently light

and long to be thrown as a spear. Hear the word is used symbolically to represent a sharp instrument of war, with which Christ will smite the nations and establish His absolutely rule.

(291) **Q.** What weapon will Christ use to subdue the earth?
A. A warrior goes into battle with his sword on his thigh. Christ's sword will be His spoken word. The word that called the world into being will call human leaders and their armies of all nations into control. Instead of a sword, on His thigh He will have written His name. "KING OF KINGS AND LORD OF LORDS."

(292) **Q.** Upon Christ's return, He will do battle with the kings of the earth (Satan's forces). Where are they located?
A. Rev.12:16-And they gathered them together to the place which is in Hebrew is called Har-Magedon (Armageddon). This will be called the battle of Armageddon, the battle of the valley of Jehoshaphat, the valley of decision, the battle of Jerusalem.

(293) **Q.** Is there really a devil?
A. Jesus said in Matt. 13:39-And the enemy who sowed them is the devil, and the harvest is the end of the age; and the reapers are the angels.

(294) **Q.** Where did Satan come from?
A. Satan is a living being. He must have been created. God created all things. In Ezek.28:15-"You were blameless in your ways From the day you were created, Until unrighteousness was found in you. Satan is God's creation.

(295) **Q.** What was Satan created for?
A. Ezek.28:14-"You were the anointed cherub who covers, And I placed you there. You were on the holy mountain of God; You walked in the midst of the stones of fire. Satan was anointed as a cherub. This implies leadership of the angelic host in the presence of the Shekinah Glory of God. He was anointed as a guardian cherub.

(296) **Q.** Where did Satan make his abode in heaven?
A. He made his abode on the holy mountain of God, where this chief cherub walked among the fiery stones.

(297) **Q.** How did Satan the anointed cherub fall?

A. Ezek.28:17 "Your heart was lifted up because of your beauty; You corrupted your wisdom by reason of your splendor. I cast you to the ground; I put you before kings, This indicates pride, pride of his beauty and wisdom that caused him to sin.

(298) **Q.** What does Satan really want to do?
A. Isaiah 14:13.14-"But you said in your heart, 'I will ascend to heaven; I will raise my throne above the stars of God, I will raise my throne above the stars of God, And I will sit on my mount of assembly In the recesses of the north. I will ascend above the heights of the clouds; I will make myself like the Most High.'"

(299) **Q.** Satan is the author of concepts like communism, liberalism, socialism and Nazism. What is the latest that sweeps America today?
A. Satan embodies all that is anti- God, anti-Christ. Who can truthfully deny that he is subverting society by destroying Christianity in order to set up his blasphemes religion headed by the anti-Christ, whom men shall worship instead of God.

(300) **Q.** There has been no other being that has caused so much misery for God's creation than Satan. Where will he end up?
A. Rev. 20:10-And the devil who deceived them was throne into the lake of fire and brimstone, where the beast and the false prophet are also; and they will be tormented day and night forever and ever.

(301) **Q.** What are the three resurrections?
A. The church age saints, the Old Testament saints, and the tribulation saints.

(302) **Q.** Satan will be bound for one thousand years. Upon his release what will he do?
A. Rev. 20:7.8-And when the thousand years are completed, Satan will be released from his prison, and will come out to deceive the nations which are in the four corners of the earth, Gog and magog, to gather them together for the war; the number of them is like the sand of the seashore.

(303) **Q.** Satan will gather his forces after his thousand year jail term. He will go after them from the four corners of the earth. What is their doom?
A. Rev.20:9-And they came up on the broad plain of the earth and surrounded the camp of the saints and the beloved city, and fire came down from heaven and devoured them.
(304) **Q.** When will the great white throne judgment take place?
A. The great white throne judgment will follow the thousand year reign.
(305) **Q.** Who will be present at the great white throne judgment?
A. Rev.20;11.12-And I saw a great white throne and Him who sat upon it, from whose presence earth and heaven fled away, and no place was found for them. And I saw the dead, the great and the small, standing before the throne, and books were opened; and another book was opened, which is the book of life; and the dead were judged from the things which were written in the books, according to their deeds.
(306) **Q.** How will the believers be judge?
A. For we must all appear before the judgment seat of Christ, that each one may be recompensed for his deeds in the body, according to what he has done, whether good or bad.
(307) **Q.** When will the believer be judged?
A. This judgments for believers will take place "in the air" following the resurrection.
(308) **Q.** What is the book of life?
A. The book of life seems to contain the names of all living people. To keep your name there one must also have his or her name written in the Lambs book of life.
(309) **Q.** What is the Lambs book of life?
A. The lambs book of is a book belonging to the Lord Jesus Christ. The Lamb's book of life includes the names of those who call on the Lamb for salvation.
(310) **Q.** What eternal dividends are there for being in the Lamb's book of life?

A. John5:24-"Truly, truly, I say to you, he who hears My word, and believes Him who sent Me, has eternal life, and does not come into judgment, but has passed out of death into life.

THE GOD OF THIS WORLD

A powerful spiritual being, named "Ahriman" (aka Satan) will incarnate in a human body. The terms "soul" "body" and "spirit" have clear meanings. Earthly and cosmically evolution is an outcome of the deeds of the gods. The central event of earth-revolution was the incarnation of Christ.

Spiritual powers are in opposition and active at this time. Lucifer, Ahriman, Sorat. Ahriman is the inspirer of materialistic science and commercialism. He permeates modern culture with deadening forces. Ordinary scientific thinking is only semiconscious. The spirits of opposition are necessary in God's evolutionary design.

Arhriman manifests at 666 intervals. Ahriman in the flesh will likely present himself as the Christ. The Christ does not reappear in a physical body, but in a super-physical ethereal form.

Ahriman can incarnate macro-cosmically in our computers. Mankind will acquire new faculties of thinking-consciousness and clairvoyance. Ahriman seeks to pervert these faculties, and to divert mankind and the earth from their destined paths in the God's evolutionary plan. Ahriman secret societies influence politics, finance, and our culture.

I wish to bring before the public some information about tremendous events approaching. I am aware that there is a lot of talk on the superhighway in this vein of thinking already. There is a general sense that something big is happening with the new millennium. I believe that this something big that is in the air is a correct perception. This is a lot of distortion that is there also. Look at this idea from the right angle.

Most of this information in this report is not new. Hell, nothing is ever new anymore. From my understanding it has been available to the public ever since the First World War. But it has not been released to the public at large. It is the public at large that needs to hear it. My mission is to make this information widely known that those who encounter it might put it to good use. I claim no special knowledge on these matters. I have just drawn on public sources and put this packet together.

If anything just think about what is written on these pages as a unique story. Take nothing for granted. Do your own research and come to your own conclusions. This vein of thinking is just another way of looking at this world. To understand the impossible situation we are in today we must approach it cosmically.

Conscientious investigations might well cause some intellectual distortions, and change the course of some ones life. This is exactly what is needed. This report needs to go viral around the world so as not to become deceived as to what is the true nature about things. We need not live in this world in deception.

I choose this subject because I am not aware of any one who is. I think it the utmost importance that this essay be distributed world wide. It can be viewed gospel as world security lies in the balance. This material is not gospel per se but it does explain things in a different light. After all, isn't that what we all seek understanding and wisdom?

The events of which I am speaking of are the approaching incarnation of a powerful, super human spiritual being, following the concomitant political, social, economic, and cultural events. Preparations for this incarnation have been building to a climax over the past four centuries or more, and the climax is approaching soon.

This being is called Ahriman. This is derived from the ancient Persian name Angra Mainyu. This name is also derived from the prehistoric Zarathustra. We might consider Ahriman to be the same being as "Satan" except that the concept "Satan" is much confused and misunderstood. Therefore, this report I will use the name "Ahriman" and will attempt to give a clearer understanding of his nature and aims than one would generally obtain.

I realize that there are many who will not take me seriously in the Christian community. I also realize that many will not take this seriously in this world. But never the less the events that will unfold will not be understood without prior knowledge. I feel that I write this at my own peril. So again I ask that you read with an open mind and heart. At least open enough to accept the concepts and thoughts.

This report is a matter of great importance; It is essential for the future of mankind and the earth that as many people as possible become wakeful and not be caught sleeping by the impending events.

SPIRIT AND SOUL

Since this report speaks of "spiritual" matters, I would like to bring into focus the concept of "spirit," along with the concepts of "soul", and "body". The "body, of course, is the physical form, perceptible by the outer senses, in the world that is usually perceived in common by people's outer senses. By "soul" I mean the inner world of subjective feelings and sensations of a man or animal. The sensations of an outer sense-perception such as green grass as well as feelings such as pleasure or pain are in the soul. Also, the inner being acts through the soul by the will, though the will is not usually conscious. We might say that the physical world acts on the soul through sensation; the soul lives in its own feelings, and acts upon the world through the will. We generally experience sensation in wakefulness, feelings as if in a dream, and will as if in deep, unconscious sleep.

In addition to living in the inner world of the soul, the man can live in the world of thought. Through thinking, we make contact with the being of the things of the world. By "spirit" I mean the essence of thought. Contrary to common misconception, thought is not subjective, but objective, in that it belongs to the whole world, accessible to all. Many people can grasp the same thought and through that thought the same objective reality, though they do not experience each others sensations and feelings. As the physical world interacts with the soul, so does the spirit; we can call forth thoughts by our acts of will, and the thoughts give us feelings.

Much of the confusion about the supposed subjectivity of thinking arises from the subjectivity of feelings and sensations connected with thinking, as well as from the fact that much of what usually passes for thinking is hardly thinking at all, but a kind of semi-conscious, automatic pseudo-thinking. In modern times, people experience thinking as if it comes, usually automatically, out of themselves, yet, thinking in essence is objective and universal. So, through our experience of thinking, we can attach an experiential, "empirical" meaning to the concept of "spirit."

All this should, of course, be taken as only a bare introduction to a vast, deep subject. For now, I am trying only to counter the widespread opinion that "soul" and "spirit" are nebulous terms. And while it is usually true that we hardly experience our thinking may be intensified so that it becomes conscious, and this development of consciousness may lead to the perception of the world and beings of soul and spirit and thus become the basis of "spiritual science."

SPIRITUAL BEINGS AND EARTHLY EVOLUTION

Following the communications of this spiritual science, I will posit that spiritual beings, known as "angels," live invisibly and involve themselves in earthly affairs. This idea has been gaining acceptance on the general culture in recent years, with a surge of interest in angels. I will also posit the existence of other spiritual beings, higher and more advanced than the angels, called the "archangels in theology or angelology.

Modern day theologians who do modern day research on angelology as angelic beings-which, taken together, are called the "hierarchies," sometimes choirs of angels," or sometimes the Gods." Some of the names given to the nine hierarchies, in ascending order, are:

ANGELS- Angeloi, Sons of Twilight, Sons of Life; all men have individual angels as guardians and carriers of their eternal selves.

ARCHANGELS-Archangeloi, Spirits of Fire; the "Folk Spirits" are of this rank.
ARCHAI-Singular "Arche"; Spirits of personality, Primal Beginnings, Principalities; the "Time Spirit" or "Zeitgeist" is of this rank.
EXUSIAI- Spirits of Form, Powers, Authorities; the "Elohim" and "Jehovah" are of this rank.
DYNAMIS- Spirits of motion, Mights, Virtues are of this rank
KYRIOTETES- Spirits of Wisdom, Dominions are of this rank.
THRONES- Spirits of will are of this rank.
CHERIBUM- Spirits of Harmony are of this rank.
SERAPHIM- Spirits of Love are of this rank.

The existence of these Hierarchical beings is mentioned in the Bible. Angels, of course, are mentioned in many places. Some other examples are: **Archangels** are mentioned in Jude 1:9. I Thes. 4:16.

Thrones, Dominions, Principalities, Powers are mentioned in Rom. 8:38; Col. 1:16; 2:15; Eph. 1:21, 3:10.

Cherubim are mentioned in Gen. 3:24; Ex. 25:18-20, 22; Num. 7:89; Ezk. 9:3, ch.10; Ps. 18:10.

Seraphim are mentioned in Isa. 6:21.

These spirits are not all "angelic," in the sense of "good and holy." Some of them, sometimes, oppose the regular, good world order. Ahriman "the unjust Prince of this world" is a "retarded" Spirit of Form, working as an Arche, opposing the good world order. Yet this opposition is not pure evil as we will see next.

Since Ahriman is a spirit of opposition, we might begin to understand his nature by understanding what he opposes: He opposes the God's plan of earthly and human development. But the situation is not as simple as a two sided contest; basic to competent understanding of the world process is the recognition of at least three kinds of spiritual influence upon the evolution of mankind and the cosmos.

We must be clear that this "evolution" is something very different from the random, meaningless, material process conceived by the Darwinist and other theorists. I mean by "evolution" a thoroughly purposeful, thought filled process of development initiated and guided by spiritual beings.

The Great Gods or the Higher Hierarchies create and nurture the evolvement of the world and mankind, so as to bring about the possibility of Men attaining the status of divinity as "Spirits of freedom and Love:- the tenth hierarchy."

At the present stage of evolution, the Man progresses through alternating periods of earth lives and purely spiritual lives: Birth, death, and reincarnation.

As the name implies, essential to the fulfillment of mankind's task is the realization of "freedom." This is meaning not so much political freedom as spiritual freedom- that Men should become independent, unique individuals acting consciously as the originators of their own deeds. Deep inner wisdom done by past individuals recently rediscovered and now being made public to help explain this evolution as being created and guided through seven great cosmic ages. We are now in the forth great age, called the "Earth" Age.

All ages' names here are given in order of succession. The previous three ages are called "Saturn," "Sun," and "Moon." Again, these are past ages of cosmic development, not to be confused with the present-day heavenly bodies of the same names. The same holds for the three future ages: "Jupiter," "Venus," and "Vulcan." The great Earth Age comprises seven lesser ages, of which we are in the fifth.

These five are called "Polarian," "Hyperborean," "Lemurian," "Atlantian," and "Post-Atlantian." And the Post-Atlantian Age comprises seven cultural epochs, of which, again, we are in the fifth. The previous four are called "Indian," "Persian," "Egypto Chaldean," and "Greco-Roman." Recorded history begins only with the EgyptoChaldean Epoch.

What is generally known of ancient Indian and Persian culture derives from records made in the third epoch. These names of epochs do not imply that nothing important was happening in other regions of the earth, but that the archetypal evolutionary impulses of the times were centered in the regions designated. The epochs last approximately 2160 years; and the present, fifth post- Atlantean epoch began about 1413AD. Neither are these epochs considered to be sharply differentiated; transitions happen gradually, future developments being prepared in advance, and past influences lingering after.

The central event of the Earth Age occurred during the Greco-Roman Epoch, in Palestine. It was the incarnation of a very high spiritual Being, a God of the normal current, called the "Christ"-culminating in the events surrounding the Crucifixion: The "Mystery of Golgatha." This event was the turning point of Earth evolution from descent from spirit into matter, toward ascent back to the spirit, with the fruits gained from sojourn into matter.

Besides the normal God's, a host of abnormal spiritual beings, called "Luciferic," also influences earthly evolution. In a sense, these oppose the normal God's plans for evolution. The Luciferic beings try to draw mankind away from the normal earth-evolution to their own abnormal psychic-spiritual cosmos of light. In the human soul they inspire pride, egotism, disinterest in one's fellow Men, fiery emotionalism subjectivity, fantasy, and hallucinations. In the human intellect they inspire generalization, unification, hypothesizing, and the building of imaginative pictures beyond reality. Human speech and thought are Lucerfic in origin; so are human self-consciousness and the capacity for independence and rebellion against the normal God's world-order. Also, susceptibility to disease originated from Luciferic influence. A high spiritual being, in a sense the leader of the Luciferic host, "Lucifer himself, incarnated in a human body, in the region of China, in the Third Millennium BC. This event brought about a revolution in human consciousness.

Before then, Men could not use the organs of intellect and lived by a kind of instinct. Lucifer was the first to grasp by the intellect the wisdom of the Mysteries theretofore revealed by the Gods to mankind in other forms of consciousness. The effects of this incarnation inspired the wisdom of Pagan culture, up through the Gnosis of the early centuries AD, and lingered even into the early 19th century.

This wisdom should not be considered to be false in itself. It is good or evil depending on who holds it and for what purposes it is used. The great Pagan initiates took it upon themselves to enter into the Luciferic influence and turn it to the good of mankind. Only through Lucerfic influence has mankind risen above the status of childishness.

Apart from Pagan culture of Nature-wisdom was the Hebraic culture, which, in a sense, separated the Man from Nature, and which prepared an hereditary current to provide a body for the incarnation of Christ. In Pagan culture the Man felt membered into the starry cosmos, without what we now know as moral impulses. Moral impulses in the human soul were prepared by Hebrewism and furthered by Christianity. Christianity is also a culmination and fulfillment of Pagan wisdom. Here "Christianity" means not so much "organized religion" as the deeds and continuing influence of the Christ-being and His hosts, not necessarily confined to formal-religious organizations.

A third spiritual influence working into human and earthly evolution is the Ahrimanic. The intention of Ahriman, and his hosts, is to freeze the earth into complete rigidity, so that it will not pass over to the Jupiter, Venus, and Vulcan ages, and to make the Man into an entirely earthly being-unindividualized, unfree, and divorced from the normal God's cosmos. The essential Ahrimanic tendency is to materialize; to crystallize; to darken; to silence; to bring living, mobile forces into fixed form- in other words, to kill that which is living.

This tendency in itself, within proper bounds is not evil; the deed, material world is necessary for the Regular God's plan of human and cosmic development. The Ahrimanic tendency is evil only when it exceeds proper bounds, when it reaches into what should be alive-and Ahirman does try to exceed proper bounds. Again, the basic reality of the world is spiritual beings together with their deeds, but Arhiman promotes the illusion, the lie, that matter is the basic reality, or the only reality. In fact, Ahrimanic spirits, not "atoms" or "ultimate particles," are the reality behind the apparently material world. Ahriman lives upon lies; he is a spirit of untruth, the father of lies.

AHRIMAN IN MODERN TIMES

In the present, fifth epoch the Ahrimanic influence in human culture is reaching a climax. The modern scientific revolution, since the 15th century, has been inspired largely by Ahriman. He is the inspirer of amoral, atheistic, mechanistic materialism, and the kind of cleverness that goes with it. The regular God's intent for the present epoch which is also called the "Consciousness Soul Epoch" is that mankind should develop increased consciousness, together with individuality and spiritual freedom that go with that consciousness.

Ahriman opposes this; he wants the Man to live from consciousness instincts as an unindividualized, impulsive animal-clever, but an animal nonetheless. Ahriman is the teacher of the lie that the Man is an animal: Darwinism had similar theories.

To the modern mind it might seem a contradiction to say Ahriman opposes increased consciousness but promotes intelligence and science. This is because the modern mind is so immured in what is generally considered to be "scientific thinking" that it has almost no conception of the true nature of conscious thinking. The fact is that "scientific" thinking normal in this epoch, no matter how clever, is hardly conscious at all, possibly with some rare exceptions at moments of "insight."

In the kind of consciousness in our scientific culture, we become conscious only of the fixed results of the thinking, after it has been accomplished; we are not usually conscious of the thinking process itself. Since it is unconscious, it is not our free action; it is automatic. When we think in the manner usual in our epoch, we are sentient automata, acting from instinct. And this is what Arhiman wants; he wants to stamp out all traces and all possibility of free, individualized human consciousness; he wants the Man not to be an individual, but only a member of a general species of pseudo-mankind-to be clever, earth bound animal, He wants Man to be homunculus.

As indicated, Ahriman is the inspirer of the most extreme kind of "scientific" materialism: The doctrine that there is no spirit or soul in the world; that life itself is not in fact alive, but is only a complex of mechanical processes; that reality is at base only quantitative, that there is no reality in the quantitative-color, sound, etc. This means even that the inner human's being is a confluence of material forces. On the emotional level, he works in the human subconscious instincts, inspiring fear, hatred, lust for power, and destructive sex impulses. On the mental level, he inspires rigid, automatic thinking; thinking almost entirely without thoughts, but thinking tremendously strongly language, in the literal words, which easily become empty words, which in turn easily become lies. This "abstract" thinking is devoid of any conscious, inner activity and devoid of any real connection to living experience, and creates a darkened consciousness without light, color, or images.

THE DEGRADATION OF LANGUAGE

It is highly characteristic of the present western culture of Ahrimanic scientism and Anglo- American economic imperialism that language has lost its instinctive spiritual meaning; that is, the connection is lost between the literal word and the spiritual impulses that constitute meaning.

Without real spiritual content, language consists only of "empty phrases," such as rule by the people, the free world, individual freedom, and so on. These phrases are largely devoid of reality in our socio-political structure; here the pervasive actuality is the power of money over Men and over life. And were the empty phrase rules in language, mere conventions-rather than living human contact-rule in social life, and mere routine-rather than lively human interest-rules in economic life.

"It is only a short step from the empty phrase to the lie." Again, this is especially true in politics and economics, for the prevalence of empty words makes possible the falsification of realities-a potent weapon in the hands of those with occult, conscious intentions to manipulate people for devious ends. In our time, people en masse act as if they are possessed by evil forces, because, in a way, they are. The demons of materialism speak through empty words. A language in which the demons of materialism have taken the place of human spiritual impulses can only lead to destruction.

I know that I am not the only one who can see these things. George Orwell was perhaps the most prominent writer to decry this trend. See, for instance, his classic essay "Politics and the English Language." He envisioned the dehumanization of language becoming deliberately intensified in the "newspeak" of the Ahrimanic nightmare 1984. Having no apparent knowledge of spiritual science, and working with only a keen observation and a love of truth, he saw what was happening in the political discourse of Western Europe and carried to the extremes in the totalitarian regimes.

In the socio-political level, the antidote for this poison of empty words is the liberation of cultural life, especially education, from political and financial power. On the individual-personal level, the antidote is the infusion of active, creative thought into language, thus creating a language in which the words point to the thoughts, evoking living thinking in the listeners. If we do not put effort into creating our original thoughts, then ready made pseudo-thoughts, trite words and phrases, come automatically to mind and carry us along with them, resulting in "thinking almost entirely without thoughts." We can at least make the effort to resist these ready made phrases and generalizations that effortlessly come to mind, and to form mental pictures of particular people, things, and events-and further, to make original word-formations describing these things and pictures from varying points of view.

The essential point is that we not let our speaking and writing be determined by unconscious influences, but that we call forth through our own efforts new, original thought-creations and convey them original, fluid, artistic word-formations. We will not always fully succeed; we are not all poets all the time; but if we consciously make this effort, then we will go far toward recovering the lost human-spirituality of language, and consequently, toward the humanization of culture. And, Not incidentally, We will thus progress toward living consciously in the thinking-free-of-literal-words that is the "language" of the spirit-soul world in which we will live after death- 'Men must learn to see through words; they will have to acquire the capacity to grasp the gesture in language."

THE AHRIMANIZATION OF CULTURE

In the social-cultural sphere, Arhiman's influence is apparent everywhere, especially strong and growing stronger throughout the later part of the 20th century and continuing at an accelerated pace still to this day. Chief among the Ahrimanic trends are:

Antagonistic nationalism based on ethnicity. Moderate folk-nationalism was a progressive principle in the past, but ethnic nationalism is retrogressive and destructive today.

Animalistic and dogmatic party politics, engendering hatred and bitterness arising from the refusal to see other, equally valid or invalid points of view.

The subjugation of our cultural life. This includes medicine, education, research and criminal jurisprudence to the political and economic power structure.

The mechanization of the political state, bound by rigid laws everywhere, with little place for free human initiative.

In every day life: Philistinism, tedium, and alienation, lack of interest in one's work, even in intellectual work. Ahriman wants knowledge to be devoid of warm human interest and connection, to be stored in libraries and not to live in human souls.

In medicine: Materialistic, mechanistic, and atrocious experimentalism and treatment, without understanding of the living human individual. The related practice of embalming corpses tends to bind the human entity to earth; this is an Ahrimanic reflection of ancient Egyptian mummification.

In social science: Blind acceptance of statistics, and the belief that the satisfaction of economic needs by itself will secure human welfare.

In economics: the subjugation of all living and human interests to the inhuman, impersonal mechanism of profit-seeking, to the "artificial person" of the corporation. In the USA this has reached such a state that the humanization influence of the labor movement is being obliterated, and the exigencies of "making a living," along with other destructive Ahrimanic trends, are destroying the human family-this in the so-called "richest country in the world."

The perspicacious American folk-wisdom has coined the term "The Almighty Dollar." The Ahrimanic "Mammon" is the archetypal god of "filthy lucre" and of the power of money over lives, as well as of all low and dark forces; his host also attack the human body and soul to corrupt and destroy them.

In the Christian religion: Narrow, simplistic interpretation of the gospels, without appreciation for the occult wisdom needed for an approach to the deep mysteries of the Christ-Being.

In literature: Books inspired directly by Ahriman, works of great intelligence that further Ahriman's goals.

In techniques: Very refined developments, but directed only at satisfying animal needs, promoting human immersion in the sense-world to the exclusion of the supersensible.

In world view: Humans as animals, animals and all living things as mechanisms, the non-existence of soul and spirit, and the non-existence of moral reality: Amoralism.

Obviously, these impulses are running amok in this world, more so all the time. They are, in fact, approaching a climax; they are preparations for the incarnation of Ahriman himself in a human body.

GOOD AND EVIL

To sum up this description of the triad of spiritual streams: The conflicts of human and spiritual life do not derive from a simple, two-sided war between good and evil. It was one of the great insights of those in the past studying these things to renew the ancient teaching of the "Golden Mean," of good as the middle way between opposing extremes.

Lucifer is too warm, too flighty, too unstable; he inspires human fanaticism, false mysticism, hot-bloodedness, and the tendency to flee earthly reality for hallucinatory pleasures.

Ahriman is too cold, too hard, too rigid, he tries to make people dry, prosaic, philistine, materialistic in thought and in deed-and hardens what would be healthy mobile, supple thoughts, feelings, and even bodies.

The Christ serves as an Exemplar of the regular God's. He represents the middle way between the two extremes. The too much and the too little; holding the opposites in balance-and leading mankind to find the healthy middle –way. Seen this way, Lucifer and Ahriman are not purely evil; they both bring to human and earthy evolution forces that are needed for good, healthy development and the fulfillment of the God's plans. Evil results only when events get out of balance and run to extremes. However, neither do Lucifer and Ahriman simply oppose each other; in a sense they work together in opposition to the God's intent for evolution; they both work to prevent mankind and the earth from progressing together to the New Jupiter.

Lucifer draws human spirits away from earthly embodiment toward his own psychic-spiritual "planet" of light; Ahriman pushes the individual human spirit out of human organism and away from the earth, so that only a hardened, mechanized, ghostly human organism, devoid of free individuality and living an instinctive-but-clever animalistic species-life remains on the hardened "cosmic slag" of the earth sounded with old moon forces.

Mankind's rightful task for the present is to lead lives of healthy, progressive, alternation between the earthly and cosmic life. The life, death, and the rebirth so as to lead earth to the New Jupiter-the profound mystery of evil is that in a higher sense, in the long run, it serves the good. This is not to imply that we would be justified in doing evil with the realization that good would result. Matt.18:7 states "Woe to the world because of its stumbling blocks! For it is inevitable that stumbling blocks come; but woe to that man through whom the stumbling block comes!

THE CHRIST

LUCIFER & AHRIMAN

The true picture of evil might be more complex than the statement above. I will make a statement that will introduce a third stream of spirits of opposition: The "Asuras." This is a borrowed Eastern term. These forces are a retarded Archai who work to destroy the human "I" or the ego itself.

The Asuras might be agents of the actual Antichrist, the Sun Demon, also known as "Sorat" (or Sorath). In some beliefs Sorat is identified as the Apocalyptic Beast 666. While it seems true that the numerological interpretation of the Hebrew spelling of "Sorat" gives the number 666, still the position of Sorat in relation to Lucifer and Ahriman is not altogether clear to this writer. A possible solution to this question might follow from the imagery of the Apocalypse: Michael casts the Dragon out of Heaven; immediately afterwards arise the two "beasts"-the first from the sea Lucifer and the second from the land Ahriman.

Lucifer and Ahriman appear on earth as two beings or principles, but they are the progeny of the one spirit of opposition-the Dragon-in heaven. If we identify the Dragon, the Antichrist, as Sorat, we can picture Lucifer and Ahriman as the left and right hands of Sorat. Christ strives to hold Lucifer and Ahriman in balance so that they serve the good of the regular God's purpose, while Sorat strives to push them out of balance, so that they work for destruction.

While Lucifer seeks to draw the human "I"-the ego to his own planet, and Ahriman seeks to harden the earth and the human organism so that no ego can live in a human on earth, Sorat-through the Asuras-seeks to destroy the Ego itself, along with the earth. Sorat uses Lucifer and Ahrimanas spirits of seduction to mask his own true intention of pure destruction. And Sorat manifests in social evolution as pure destruction, especially in the wars and mass murders of our time.

Now the true picture might look something like The Christ is Controlling Lucifer, Ahriman, and Sorat at bay until the end of the age then He will let them loose to bring about the end of the ages by Apocalyptic means.

WHEN AND WHERE

It is believed in some inner circles that the Ahrimanic incarnation will happen in the West sometime in the Third Millennium. In this nomenclature "west" means primarily Britain and the English speaking America. There is ample reason to suspect that the destined place for this event is North America, for the effect of the American natural environment on the human body and soul especially favors Ahrimanic tendencies. According to some insights, each of the various regions of the earth has its unique effect upon the human organism. In America, the Ahrimanic influence is strong, rising from the center of the earth, carried by electromagnetism. This strengthens the entity known as the human "double" or "Doppelganger."

The Doppelganger is an Ahrimanic soul-being with intelligence and will, feeling, but with no individual, spiritual ego and tending to bind the human soul to the body, hardening human thinking, feeling, and willing. All Men have a Doppelganger living in their nerve-electricity. Infusing into their souls all sorts of degrading, depressing impulses, as well as instigating internal illnesses. Electricity is the "sub-natural," rigidifying shadow of soul forces. The Ahrimanic tendencies in America are well known even to those whose perception is unenlivened by occult knowledge. American culture has long been famous for its violence and hard-boiled materialism, and its degeneracy and decadence.

As to the time and when there is no one that can say for sure. Only the regular God can say for certainty. No one knows the time or the hour. There is a consensus that it will happen by the end of the third millennium. In other circles they believe sometime in the middle of the third millennium. In even more extreme thinking it is believed that by the end of the 20th century we will see the beginning of the Apocalypse, but this obviously is not the case. But what ever you believe we are starting to experience a Great Crises in the world. By the end of the 20th century it is believed that a "War of All against All," will take place. This is when mankind might well "stand at the grave of civilization."

In any case, it seems highly likely that a major onslaught- either the incarnation or birth of Ahriman himself, or the advent of the "false prophet" of the Apocalypse, or some other attack- occurs around the turn of the 20th century. To see why this is so, we need to do a few simple calculations, based on occult principle of meaningful rhythms in history. Let the skeptical reader be a true skeptic and suspend judgment, and take in the following discussion with a mind open to possibilities unsuspected by the materialistic mind.

SOME OCCULT HISTORY

Unknown to history, but while the incarnation of Christ was happening in Palestine, another stupendous drama was played out in Mexico. A high initiate of the negative Mysteries, the most advanced "black magician in the world, had reached, by repeated ritual murders of an especially horrible kind, the threshold of knowledge of certain deep, cosmic secrets. This knowledge would have give him the ability, as was his intention, of achieving the Ahirmanic goals of completely rigidifying the earth, so as to draw it out of the progressive development toward the New Jupiter, and of binding human organisms as automata in that "slag" of the earth.

He was thwarted in this intention by the incarnate high Sun-Being "Vitzliputzli," who caused the black magician to be crucified at the same time as the Crucifixion of Jesus Christ-a shattering reflection in the American continent of the Events in Palestine. Since then the soul of this black magician has been held in a kind of "prison."

Recall that the Greco-Roman Epoch ran approximately 2160 years, from 747 BC to 1413 AD. The mid point of this epoch was 1413 AD minus 2160/2=333 AD. Consider the Occult teaching that events in history occur at times that, as it were, reflect and balance the events equidistant in time from a midpoint. Taking 333 AD as the midpoint, the fulcrum of the balance, and on one side the birth in Palestine, on the other side of the scales would be 333 AD+333=666AD. The big event, known to history, of the 7th century was the rise of Islam. Another event, not so famous but still known to history, was the transfer of ancient Greek philosophy, especially Aristotle's works, probably including the lost work of alchemy to the Academy of Jundi Sabur near present day Baghdad.

Following the expulsion of the philosophers from Syrian Edessa in 489 AD and from Athens in 529 AD, the philosophers had found refuge in what was then the Persian Empire, and at that Academy they pursued their calling. Then this knowledge passed to the Islamic Arabs, and science of a particular bent reached a high development under them, while Europe was in the "Dark Ages." Only gradually, over many centuries, did this science pass over to Europe, where it developed into modern scientific revolution. Again, the trend of modern science, as it has in fact developed, is Ahrimanic. The direct ancestor of scientific materialism was this Arabian science, which was itself derived from the Academy of Jundi Sabur. Thus, on the other side of the 333AD midpoint from the birth in Palestine was the rise of an active materialistic, anti-Christian worldview in Jundi Sabur.

Occult history reveals how this came about: Sorat intended to approach physical manifestation in 666 AD at Jundi Sabur, and to bestow upon the philosophers there a super-human knowledge. This knowledge was to consist of everything that mankind, under the plan of the regular God's, was to learn through its own efforts by the height of the present, Consciousness Soul Epoch.

This epoch began in 1413 AD, so its midpoint will be 2493 AD. In other words, Sorat wanted to give to mankind, prematurely and without the requisite human effort and experience, the knowledge that would be right and healthy for mankind to achieve through work and evolution by the middle of the Third millennium.

The regular God's plan for the Consciousness Soul Epoch is for mankind to acquire, through self-education and self discipline, the free, conscious, individualized human personality. If the mankind of the 7th century had been given this advanced knowledge at that immature stage of development, when people could not think in full consciousness, the result would have been disastrous. Just consider how much evil mankind has done with the science we have acquired up to now, at our present stage of maturity or immaturity, and then try to imagine what the relatively primitive people of the 7th century would have done with the science of 2493 AD.

This picture is bad enough, but we need to recall the Occult insights to begin to get the whole picture. If Sorat had succeeded, we humans would have lost the possibility of developing our true nature, and would have become egotistic, animalistic automata, with no possibility of further development. Would have been earth bound, and the Earth could never then pass over to the Jupiter, Venus, and Vulcan stages.

The normal God's plan would have been thwarted and Men could not become the Spirits of Freedom and Love. However, the rise of Islam thwarted this plan of Sorat. It is a deep, mysteries paradox that Islam, which was, and is, opposed to Christianity in many ways, also in effect worked jointly with the

Christ-impulse in history, by blanketing, by "skimming the cream off," this Sorat science, and by watering it down. Still, this science survived, and has worked on into the present day, but the worst was averted, for those times. The weakened Jundi Sabur impulse, as a distorted Quasi-Aristotelianism, passed to the Arabs, over Africa and Spain, to France, England, and through the monasteries and then brought back over the continent.

The "Realism" of the Medieval scholastics opposed this Arabian influence, somewhat correctly seeing it is inimical to Christianity; but with the decline and decadence of Medieval Aristotelianism, and with the dawn of modern, anti-Aristotolian "empiricism," the diluted, but still powerful, Sorat science came to dominate world-culture.

BRUTAL AND SPIRITUAL SCIENCE

The father of death science has said, propounding scientific experimentalism, that we must put Nature on the rack and force her to answer the questions we put to Her. This figure will speak volumes to those who meditate upon it: We, seeking information for whatever motives, are to torture the Goddess who gave us birth and nurture, so as to cause Her, through unbearable pain and injury, to blurt out secrets which She, in her wisdom, conceals from the impure and self-seeking. In much of so called "physiological research" and "medical training" this is hardly even a metaphor; the torture unto death is quite literal. The usual victims are animals, but all too many "researchers" are not above using human "subjects" when they can get enough power over them. And even a slight whiff of Occult knowledge shows us a deeper meaning: The central rite of "Satanism" or black magic"-sometimes crude, sometimes sophisticated-is the deliberate, ritual torture and killing of animals and, at a more advanced level, of humans. When done is a precise way, this practice confers knowledge and power upon the practitioner; also, it affects the whole earth, hardening and rigidifying it, to the characteristic Ahrimanic purpose. Thus we can see the hordes of "researchers" and medical students- who hurt, injure, and "sacrifice" animals-as undergoing an unconscious, Ahrimanic black magic initiation, which hardens, brutalizes, and Ahrimanizes their souls, and through them also the culture, and even the earth itself.

Sacrifice is the actual word they commonly use, not thinking which "god" they sacrifice unto. Vivisection is truly the archetypal act of modern science as it is generally understood and practiced.

In contrast, to our brutal science there does exist a little known scientific trend. The scientific method is quite different from the brutal Ahrimanic mode and likewise it is illustrated by using a metaphor. It goes like this:

We must approach Nature as a reverent lover, and, perhaps, She will whisper to us Her intimate secrets. The contrast to the brutal Ahrimanic mode could hardly be more stark. Also, the brutal method of scientific investigation, in contrast to amoral experimentalism, is a method of self-improvement and self-development-a reverent meditating upon the facts of experience, in the hope that they will speak. This scientific method has, of course, been all but buried under the Ahrimanic avalanche.

Spiritual science sees soul and spirit in Nature, in a real, practical way, completely consistent with the "empirical" facts. It reverently approaches the scientific laboratory as a holy place, and the experiment as a sacrament, as a revelation of the Creator-Spirits through the sacred symbols of Nature. This is consistent only with the moral development of the scientist, and with the furtherance of the God's plan of human and cosmic evolution.

666 AGAIN

The year 666 rhythm continued further; another period ended in 1332 AD. Around this time 1312, the cruel suppression of the Knights Templar began. Little is known to history of the true nature of the Templars, because of their secretive nature and the distortions passed to history by their triumphant enemies.

But these Knights did cultivate an esoteric Christianity that, although somewhat flawed, had the potential of bringing about a more humane civilization in Europe. This possibility was thwarted by the power of the French King, Philip the Fair, and his allies in the Church. Philip, through the torture and killing of the Templars, and through the material inspiration from their looted gold, attained a kind of Ahrimanic initiation-knowledge, but he died soon thereafter.

The Templars were either killed or driven underground, and Medieval culture declined until the Renaissance and reformation. The Templar-impulse did continue underground, to pass over to the "Lodges," especially York and Scottish Rite Freemasonry. These Lodges worked in opposition to Roman-Catholicism, at least until the 18th century, when Freemasonry and esoteric-political Catholicism united in opposition to Napoleon, but the esoteric content of Freemasonry became decadent and Ahrimanized.

Nevertheless, many of the modern institutions of "liberal republican democracy" such as freedom of speech, religion, and the press are very largely due to the influence of Freemasonry, especially in the USA.

And, of course, another 666 year cycle ended around 1998AD. As stated already, it is apparent that the Ahrimanic influence in culture is building to some kind of climax. Indeed, as is obvious to all with eyes to see, that civilization in the USA, despite the triumphant march of technology, human culture and civilization are decaying regardless of erstwhile "rising economic indicators". It is an easy guess that decades after 1998 AD are a propitious period for a major Ahrimanic manifestation: Perhaps the appearance of Ahriman himself; or since 1998=3x666 years since Birth of the body for the incarnation of Christ, perhaps the body was born which is to be the vehicle for Ahriman, possibly 30 years later; or perhaps some other major event, such as the advent of the "false Prophet" of the Apocalypse.

TRUE AND FALSE

These are approximate times only; the outer effects of Occult hidden events may manifest only gradually. In 1998 we did not see newspaper headlines announcing a spectacular, "supernatural" event. But if we had been alive in 666 AD or 1332 AD neither would we have likely been informed by the then contemporary analogues of headlines that any major, "supernatural" events had occurred.

Those manifestations of evil did not fully succeed according to the "plan"; other influences intervened and moderated the outcomes. The Occult machinations were hardly known to the public.

Such may also be true in the present: The actual course of events depends on many contending forces and upon consciousness and will of Men; and the crux of the struggle will likely be hidden to the wide public. We will live and or die in the outer effects of the Occult causes, as uncomprehending as is usual in social cataclysms. This essay is an attempt to lessen the incomprehension, and to lighten the mental atmosphere of this planet, even a little. Surely, as "thoughts are things," even a slight change in consciousness can influence physical events in the right direction.

As in the turn of every Millennium: every 1000 years Lucifer and Ahriman work together with special power. They will never give up.

A cynic might say that these predictions allow for plenty of" wiggle room" for the incarnation of Ahriman: 1998 to the first part of the new millennium, or even the end of this millennium. I will concede that the time is not very precise, but I believe nevertheless that it is highly likely that this incarnation will manifest in the next few years to half century or century. Even without occult insight, one who observes the present social and cultural changes approaching.

Again, it is not certain that Ahriman's incarnation will be immediately known to the public; Occultist warns that Ahriman wants mankind to be unconscious of his true nature and to see his advent as progressive and good for human welfare.

"If Ahriman were able to slink into a humanity unaware of his coming, that would gladden him most of all. It is for this reason that the occurrences and trends in which Ahriman is working for his future incarnation must be brought to light."

Ahriman will establish a possible secret school for powerful "magic" arts and clairvoyance. The technical applications of this highly intelligent spirit will indeed look like "magic" to us, even as advanced as we might consider our science to be-for Ahriman's understanding is not limited by the crude materialism he foists upon mankind. And the clairvoyance bestowed upon Ahriman's pupils will be effortless, not won through the legitmate occultism. It will give spirit-vision, but the visions will be subjective and deceptive; people will see differing, conflicting visions of the soul and spirit worlds, and will fall into confusion and conflict.

Ahriman-in-the-flesh will be an overwhelming powerful and impressive figure, when he reveals himself. And it seems probable that, as the Father of Lies, he will present himself as that which he is most certainly not: Christ, in His Second Coming. And again, it is America, where many religious people, which will be especially susceptible to Ahriman's deceptions. It is entirely possible that they who cling to the Gospels with a superficially literalistic interpretation closed to occult insight will be the very people who will be the false Christ's followers.

THE TRUE SECOND COMING

Another tremendous revelation from the Occults spiritual science concerns the true nature of the second coming of Christ. The Occult is adamant that the physical incarnation of Christ can happen once and only once. "Just as a pair of scales can have only one balancing point, so in Earth evolution the event of Golgatha can take place only once."

The amazing fact is that the Second Coming is happening now, that most of mankind is unaware of it. Actually, the term "second coming" is not in the New Testament; the Greek word is parousia, meaning roughly "active presence."

It was this "presence" that Saul/Paul experienced on the road to Damascus; Paul being mankind's "premature birth" of the coming new experience of Christ.

Parousia was translated into Latin as adventus, which means arrival, thus helping to give rise to the expectation of a physical arrival of Christ. The original Greek term seems in agreement or harmony with the Scriptures explanation. In fact, it is the driving force behind the "Apocalyptic" convulsions and struggles of our time.

For, as the picture is given in the Apocalypse of John, the bottomless pit is opened, Michael casts the Dragon and his host onto the earth, the vials of wrath are poured out, and Babylon is over thrown-all in preparation for Christ's triumph that brings the New Heaven and the New Earth.

"Ethereal" means the system of "formative forces," bordering on the physical that raises inert matter to the realm of the living. Plants, animals, and humans all have ethereal, formative- force "bodies," and when the ethereal body forsakes the physical body, the physical body becomes ordinary matter; in other words, it dies. The earth, being the body of a living Being, also has a formative-force body, the "ethereal earth." These ethereal forces manifest especially in whether phenomena, such as cloud formation. It is a false, Ahrimanic science that sees cloud formation as a merely material process of evaporation and condensation of "water molecules"; this is rather a process of de-materialization and re-materialization through the workings of the ethers.

With these concepts, we see new meaning in the Bible versus concerning the Ascension and Return of Christ. A cloud received Him out of their sight. Acts1:9. This seems to be saying that Christ ascended into the ethereal, formative- force region of the earth. And the statement that "He shall come back in this manner as you have seen Him go into Heaven" Acts 1:11 seems to say that He shall return from the ethereal regions: "Behold He cometh in clouds" Rev. 1:7. The belief here is that the Christ shall not come again in the flesh seems to be in harmony with the Bible: "Then if any man shall say to you, look, here is the Christ, of look there is the Christ. Believe it not He does not come in the desert or secret chambers nor any place else on earth."

On the contrary, the Second Coming shall be a tremendous event, not limited to a particular location: "For as lightening comes out of the east, and shines onto the west; so shall the coming of man be," Matt. 44:27.

The ethereal is super-physical, not bound by the laws of material space; Christ's appearance in the ethereal earth is everywhere-at-once. And since the ethereal is super-physical, some degree of super-physical vision, or "clairvoyance," is needed to see into it.

Few people at the present stage of evolution have that kind of clairvoyance, and some may have it sporadically. But the Second Coming is only the beginning: true clairvoyance, as opposed to the deceptive Ahrimanic clairvoyance will reveal to consciousness the ethereal Christ in the centuries to come.

Ahriman dreads human consciousness of the ethereal Christ, and fights against it. It is essential for us to grasp the fact that he who shall come in the flesh is not Christ, but Ahriman: "For there shall arise false Christs, and false prophets, and shall show great signs and wonders" Matt. 44:24.

The Occult reveals the notion that since the beginning of the present reign of the Sun-Archangel Michael as the Time Spirit in 1879 AD, the human ethereal body is becoming less closely bound to the physical body, thus opening the possibility of new clairvoyance.

In 1933 AD, which is the two 950-year cycles of the precession of the nodes of Saturn since the Crucifixion and Resurrection in 33 AD, would have been an especially propitious time for the beginning of widespread perception of the ethereal Christ.

But this was hindered by the rise to power of Hitler-one expression of Sorat himself "rising from the Abyss"-and by the many convulsions and distractions around the same time in earth-life. What was hindered in 1933 might again become propitious around 2000-2100 AD. This is a reflection of the calling of Abraham around 2000-2100 BC. We may speculate that Ahriman and Sorat will oppose this new Christ-consciousness by even more horrendous hindrances.

OCCULT MEANING OF THE COMPUTER

This very interesting theory interprets the progressive mechanization of culture not only as an Ahrimanic influence, but as the actual "macrocosmic incarnation" of Ahriman: this is being brought to completion through the development of the electronic computer. We can trace the milestones in the evolution of the computer as reflections of the spiritual events in the heavens.

For example, in the 1840's, around the time of Jehovah's abandonment of human blood-bound thinking to Ahriman, Boolean algebra was developed. The year 1879-the time of Michael's accession as Time Spirit and the final expulsion of the "Dragon" onto earth- saw the publication of Frege's Begriffschrift, a great milestone in the development of "formal logic": the separation of logic from the spiritual "Word."

Also in 1879: Edison invented the electric light. Light is separated from the sun and plunged into the "sub-earthly": Electricity is Ahrimanic "light".

Trotsky and Stalin were born: Merganthalar invented the Linotype machine; Bessemer introduced the hard-steel process; and the U.S. Census Bureau hired Hermin Hollerith, who developed the first large-scale punched-card tabulating machine.

The Christ's "coming in the clouds" was reflected on earth in the early 1930's by the publication of Godel's "incompleteness theorem," which demonstrated that a truly-thinking machine is impossible, but which also led to the development of "recursion theory," which is the essential conceptual framework for "artificial intelligence", and "artificial life."

Also in 1930, by a fortuitous comedy of error, the planet Pluto was discovered. Pluto, of course, is the god of the underworld, and the discovery of "his" planet was a synchronistic harbinger of the unleashing of the sub-material "powers of the pit" upon earth: later transits of Saturn and Uranus to Pluto's discovery position marked the bombing of Hiroshima and the explosion of the first H-bomb.

In addition to this it is well known that the development of the electronic computer proceeded exponentially, from Von Neumann's development of the "stored program" to the desktop and the laptop. A lesser known development was the "Josephson effect," which allow as the construction of semi-conductors from superconducting materials. Thus, electrical circuits can operate without "Luciferic" heat, and Ahriman, whose nature is " freezing cold," can completely enter into electrical devices. As superconducting computers became more common, Ahrimanic beings higher than "elements" might actually incarnate in them, since no physical energy is consumed in a superconducting circuit. Ahrimanic "elemental spirits" inhabit our artificial machines, just as normal "elementals" or nature spirits": gnomes, undines, sylphs, salamanders work in and throughout the living processes of nature. It can be summed up: Sunless light and wordless logic intertwined, and out of them came the computer." Thus, while Ahriman incarnates "microcosmically" in a human body, we might also face the "macrocosmic" literal incarnation of Ahriman in our machines.

AN EVOLUTIONARY LEAP

The incarnation of high spiritual beings in human bodies has the special significance that new possibilities for human development are opened up, because, as it were, the way is cleared by these high-spiritual-beings-in-the-flesh being the first to accomplish these developments.

Lucifer was the first to use the organs of intellect. Christ was the first to redeem the "fallen" death-prone human body with the Resurrection Body. Likewise, Ahriman-in-the-flesh will try to inaugurate a new human capacity, for his own ends: He wishes to bring the shadowy, braid-bound, semi-conscious, clever Ahrimanic "thinking" into the human ethereal body. This would be an especially evil development if it is carried into the average human organism. It is normal and healthy, at the present stage of human evolution, for the human ethereal body to dissolve into the wide cosmos in the days immediately following death. This, of course happens after one's life passes before one's eyes.

After words the human soul-spirit entity rises to higher regions, where it is purified and prepared for a new earth-life. But materialism in the earth-life hardens the ethereal body so that it does not dissolve, but remains near the earth for a longer time, while the dead human entity serves Ahriman. Only slowly and in unconsciousness do such dead spirits enter the spirit-worlds to prepare for a new incarnation.

Ahriman wishes to be the first to so harden the ethereal so that it becomes the vehicle of automatic, intellectual thinking-devoid-of-will, and thus to make it possible to keep humans ethereal bodies permanently in the region of the earth. Then the earth would become so hardened that it would not pass over to the Jupiter Age, and humans would become clever, animalistic, ghostly, earth-bound creatures. The God's plan for human and earthly evolution would be thwarted.

Let's look at it this way:"Ahriman works against the Word 'Heaven and Earth shall pass away, but My Words shall not pass away." He wills that the words shall be thrown away, that heaven and earth shall continue on." Here we get a glimpse into the motives of the sophisticated "Satanist" or black magicians." Ahriman's acolytes seek a kind of "immortality" in the slag-earth-surrounded-with-Old-Moon-forces, but the immortality with egotistic, earthly consciousness instead of the cosmic consciousness of the individualized spiritual ego.

The regular God's intend that in the present epoch people should indeed think free of the physical brain, but with free, conscious, self created thinking. This development would gradually open the possibility of the reintegration of mankind into the spiritual cosmos, and further the passing of the earth over to the New Jupiter. Mankind could eventually rise to the rank of Spirits of Freedom and Love, and not sink to the level of earth-bound, animalistic, clever automata. To put it mildly: There is a lot at stake here.

TURNING EVIL TO GOOD

But Ahriman's incarnation need not be an evil event, as he wishes it to be. This incarnation is necessary in human and earthly evolution, and it can be turned toward the good, It humankind meets it in the right way: On the mundane level, we can remedy Ahrimanic tedium in the work-life and the intellectual life, by filling them with warm, Luciferic enthusiasm, by finding what is interesting in them, by getting ourselves interested in objective, impersonal facts and processes. On the psychological level, we can remedy Luciferic subjectivity and fiery emotionalism by observing ourselves coolly, as we would an external natural process.

On a higher level, we can become more aware of the meaning of our own lives, and of the world-process, by studying and filling ourselves with the modern form of cosmic wisdom, given by spiritual science. This is a renewal of wisdom that was formerly kept hidden, or "occult" in the mysteries. Today it is essential that more of this wisdom become generally known, if human culture is not succumb to Ahriman.

Just as the ancient initiates entered into Lucerfic wisdom and rescued it for the good of mankind, now must mankind, with the consciousness gained from spiritual science and from the ethereal Christ, enter into the coming Ahrimanic knowledge and turn it to good purpose. The Ahrimanic knowledge will show what cleverness can, and cannot, produce from earthly forces.

If we meet Ahriman consciously, we can acquire through him the realization that the Earth is becoming old and must decline physically, eventually to die and enter the spiritual worlds, to be reborn as the New Jupiter. And through this decline, humankind is to be lifted above the earthly, as the seed survives the dying plant in winter, only to sprout and grow again in the spring

THE EPOCH OF CONSCIOUSNESS

The fundamental principal in this, the Consciousness Soul Epoch, is the emergence in the Man of conscious, individualized, independent thinking. Concurrent with the emergence of this soul-force, as a by product as it were, are wider possibilities for the workings of the forces of Death and Evil. But these workings are, as in the character of Ahriman, so falsified that, for example, the cultural institutions that are generally regarded as most beneficial-education and medicine- are in fact among the worst carriers of evil, not to imply that these institutions should be shunned or destroyed, but purified and renewed-in part by their liberation from money and politics. When this epoch has run its course, which means if it will have fulfilled its potential, human culture will be vastly different. For example, the distinction between "civilized" and "primitive" peoples will have been erased, and a kind of moral "socialism" will have become instinctive.

Our specific task for the Consciousness Soul Epoch is to acquire three great truths, the same truths Sorat wished to foist upon mankind in the 7th century, with his own slant. We might presume that Ahriman-in-the-flesh will likewise try to insert them into our own culture and distort them to his own ends. It is a task of an alert and conscious mankind, schooled in spiritual science and led by the Christ, to gain these three truths through our own striving and to use them for the good development of the earthly creation.

The first truth concerns the mystery of Birth and Death: The human soul in physical world has but the semblance of the true soul-life that it had before conception and will have again after death. The life in the sense-world interrupts the supersensible soul-life in the world-between-death-and-rebirth, so that we can gain, for the spirit, that which can be gained only in the sense-world. To see this truth, we must "look Lucifer in the eye," and thus see through the distortions and illusions he spreads over the human soul.

The destiny of the "East", meaning the Slavic regions and eastwards, is to give rise to a "eugenic occultism": The knowledge of how, through astrological regulation of conception, to bring the right human entities to birth at the right time and place for forward evolution, or conversely, to bring in the wrong entities, for hindrance of right evolution. Thus, this eugenic occultism can cause great good or great harm, depending on how it is used.

The second truth concerns the Mystery of the Body: that the human body is not a lump of matter, but a form, which is spiritual in origin, and through which interchanging substances are constantly in flux. This knowledge will lead to a true medical art, the essence of which is to keep intact the natural healing forces of the body. The destiny of the "Middle" meaning Central Europe is to give rise to this "hygienic occultism"- which, of course, can lead to great good, but can also cause great harm if it is used without strict conscientiousness.

The third truth concerns the Mystery of Matter: That the reality behind "material substance" is not "atoms," or "molecules," neither is it "ultimate particles," but is spirit-to be exact:" Ahrimanic spirits, in rhythmic inter-relations. The true picture of "solid matter" is not a machine, but a rainbow: A ghostly appearance, an outcome of spiritual process. Modern physics, in some advanced theorizing, may have made some halting moves towards this truth, but the dead mechanistic world-conception still holds sway over the science which dominates world-culture. This scientism is the Ahrimanic lie, the descendant of the Jundi Sabur influence, which, even though weakened, banished soul and spirit from the world view.

To see through this lie, we must "look Ahriman in the eye"-a dangerous undertaking if we are not prepared by spiritual science. The destiny of the West, meaning primarily the English speaking world, is to give rise to a "mechanistic occultism." This will bring about more fantastic machine forces, based on rhythm and resonance. But the introduction of such machine forces would cause harm to society if the political, cultural, and economic spheres are not made mutually independent, and if egotism is not banished from the economy.

Ahriman seeks to divert and pervert these three destined developments of the Consciousness Soul Epoch, through the activity of angels who rejected the Christ influence during the Egypto-Chaldean Epoch. In the present times, the "Christian" angels pour pictures of spirit-realities into the deep regions of the human soul-organism. If the Man does not take up these pictures consciously, they sink down into the ethereal body and act as unconscious instincts through the influence of the Ahrimanic angels. These unconscious instincts work against the three progressive evolutionary trends in the following ways:
1. Perverting the Eugenic Occultism, destructive sex impulses affect the whole social life, working against the development of conscious human brotherhood, and making a mankind entirely egotistical and entirely controlled by instinctive urges carried in the blood.
2. Perverting the Hygienic Occultism, medicine becomes materialistic and can be used to heal or harm, according to egotistic purposes.
3. Perverting the Mechanistic Occultism, powerful, Keely-like machine forces are employed, controlled not by the "vibrations" of good people, seeking liberation of the workers, but by egotistic people for the evil purpose of attaining power and control over the masses.

The first two perversions are readily apparent in modern society; the third has yet to emerge in public. Again, the direction that these trends of the present epoch will take depends upon human consciousness and will.

SOME OCCULT POLITICS

Some powerful, Ahrimanic secret societies linked to the Lodges in Britain and the USA strive to keep their version of this third truth, of the spirituality of matter, as their own secret and to ensure that the wider public knows a crude atheistic-mechanistic scientism, in which spirit and soul have no place. In more recent times, one can notice that the "crude materialism" given to the public is beginning to be replaced by a more quasi-esoteric materialism.

These societies also strive to guide political and economic trends over the world so that the budding potentialities of the Middle and Eastern peoples come under their domination. The history of modern times has a very largely been the story of the out-workings of this struggle.

The crimes of the secret Anglo-American power groups include the instigation of the First World War and the consequent establishment of the Bolshevik regime in the East. These power groups believe that the English-speaking peoples are destined to justifiably dominate the East Slavs in this, the fifth cultural epoch, for the purpose of guiding their nascent potentialities, which should blossom to lead the world-culture in the sixth epoch-just as the Romans, during the forth epoch, dominated by Britain for her future leadership in the fifth epoch.

Some truth does lie behind this concept: this is the epoch of the consciousness soul, and the English-speaking peoples are gifted to develop the consciousness soul in an instinctive way, and it is true that the Slavs are destined to lead world-culture in the sixth epoch. But these power groups seek, through illegitimate means, to guide toward illegitimate, Ahrimanic ends these inherent potentialities, which are loosely "written into" destiny.

Many historians and " paranoid right-wing conspiracy nuts" have, solely through common sense and open eyed observation of external events, discerned some of the out-workings of the influence of these secret societies through their semi-secret instruments; The Council on Foreign Relations, The Order of the Skull and Bones. These have members that include George Bush, Averell Harriman, and an amazing number of powerful Americans, The Rhodes Scholarships, The Round Table, etc.

But these observers, lacking in occult knowledge, can only guess at the true aims of the secret power groups. The "Anglophile" societies may disagree among themselves about means and details, but essentially they aim to gain world-domination for themselves, though certainly not for the good of the masses of the English-speaking peoples, and to influence all cultural trends in an Ahrimanic direction.

Now, in "post cold war" Europe, the Anglo-Americans and the Jesuit-Catholic power groups apparently are working together to make the basic arrangements of this part of the "New World Order": Central Europe, from France to Poland, is to be dominated by the Jesuit interests, while the "East", meaning roughly the regions historically Orthodox Christian, is to be dominated by the Anglo-American "West." This arrangement furthers the aims the Anglo-Americans by preventing cultural collaboration between Central Europe and the Eastern Slavs, thus preventing the rise of a strong, healthy and independent Central Europe culture that could meditate and balance the East and the West.

This the present push toward the "New World Order" in Europe is a continuation of the long-standing Anglo-American policy of obliterating Central Europe, especially Germany, as a political and cultural force and of controlling the future seeds being prepared in East-Europe the same policy that led to First World War and the Bolshevik Revolution.

The deeper, Ahrimanic aim of the Anglo-Americans is to defeat the God's plan for Earth-evolution, by turning Earth into a heap of dark, frozen, cosmic slag, haunted by an earthbound mankind of ghostly homunculi-and to secure for themselves a privileged place in this Ahrimanic world-order: This is Ahrimanic immortality, with earthly consciousness and power over the uninitiated.

But much depends on us. We need to become conscious of these power groups, as well as their deeper aims and the aims of Ahriman himself. If we do not acquire this alert consciousness, Ahriman might have his way, and the future of the earth, and of humankind, will be dark and bleak.

The earth's future, as well as our own, is our responsibility. Any real progress toward a healthy social order depends on mankind's development of a new kind of thinking. The present, Ahrimanic, brain-bound pseudo-thinking is inherently anti-social; It subconsciously tries to dominate other people and put them to sleep. Most present anti-social aspects of society proceed from anti-social consciousness; the brain-bound pseudo-thinking is determined by subjective, unconscious instincts, not by concurrence with the objective truth, not by the meaning-process of the thinking itself. An anti-social society is a physical picture of the anti-social human consciousness. If human consciousness becomes harmonious with objective reality, then a truly social society will be possible. Again, it all depends on human consciousness and will.

THE ENOCHIAN APOCALYPSES

A SAINT AND A ROGUE

Between the years 1583 and 1589 the Elizabethan scholar John Dee (1527-1608) conducted a series of ritual communications with a set as discarnate entities who eventually came to be known as the Enochian angels. It was Dee's plan to use the complex system of magic communicated by the angels to advance the expansionist policies of his sovereign, Elizabeth the First. At the time England lay under the looming shadow of invasion from Spain. Dee hoped to control the hostile potentates of Europe by commanding the tutelary spirits of their various nations.

Dee was a thoroughly remarkable man. Not only was he a skilled mathematician, astronomer and cartographer, he was also the private astrologer, counselor and some believe confidential espionage agent of Queen Elizabeth. His father had been a gentleman sewer at the table of Henry VIII. When Elizabeth ascended to the throne, Dee was asked to set as auspicious date for her coronation ceremony. Always intensely loyal to Elizabeth, he had earlier been accused although falsely of trying to kill her predecessor, Bloody Queen Mary, with sorcery. His intellectual brilliance and skill as a magician were famous, and infamous, throughout Europe.

In his occult work he was aided by an equally extraordinary person, Edward Kelly (1555-1597), the son of a Worcester apothecary, who dreamed of discovering the secret of the philosopher's stone and dabbled in the black art of necromancy. Fleeing Lancaster in 1580 on charges of forging title deeds, Kelly found it prudent to set out on a walking tour of Wales. Somewhere near Glastonbury he purchased a portion of the fabled red powder that could turn base metals into gold from an innkeeper who had received it from tomb robbers.

Dee was a saint and Kelly was a rogue, but they were bound together by their common fascination for ceremonial magic and the wonders it promised. Dee possessed little talent for medium ship. He tried to overcome this limitation by hiring a mountebank named Barnabas Saul as his professional scryer but had poor results. When he learned of Kelly's considerable psychic abilities, he eagerly employed Kelly as his seer for the sum of 50 pounds per annum.

Dee invoked the Enochian angels to appearance within a scrying crystal or a black mirror of obsidian by means of prayers and certain magical seals. After Kelly alerted Dee to the presence of the spirits, Dee questioned them. Kelly reported their sayings and doings back to Dee, who recorded their words and actions in his magical diaries.

The most important portion of Dee's transcription of the Enochian communications, covering the years 1582-1587, was published in London in 1659 by Meric Casaubon under the title a true and faithful Relation of What passed for many years between Dr. John Dee and Some Spirits. This fascination work has been reprinted several times in recent decades and is readily available.

The spirits got their name from the nature of the system of magic they described to Dee. It was, they claimed, the very magic that Enoch the Patriarch had learned from the angels of heaven. The angel Ave tells Dee: Now hath it pleased God to deliver this Doctrine again out of darkness: and to fulfill his promise with thee, for the books of Enoch. Compared to it, the angels asserted to Kelly, all other forms of magic were mere playthings.

Although Dee faithfully recorded all the details Enochian magic in his diaries, he never tried to work this system in any serious way. We cannot know the reason with certainty. His rupture in 1589 from Kelly, who stayed on in Bohemia to manufacture gold for the emperor Rudolph the Second whole Dee returned to England at the request of Elizabeth, may have inconvenienced his plans. However, it is my contention, as I shall demonstrate below, that Dee was awaiting permission from the angels to employ their magic, and this permission was not given in his lifetime.

THE REALITY OF THE ENOCHIAN ANGELS

It is necessary to state here unequivocally for those unfamiliar with Enochian magic that neither Dee nor Kelly fabricated the spirit communications. Both believed completely in the reality of the angels, although they differed about the motives of these beings. Dee believed the angels obedient agents of God submissive to the authority of Christ. Kelly mistrusted them and suspected them of deliberate deception. The dislike was mutual. The angels always treated Kelly with amused contempt. Kelly hoped the angels would communicate the secret of the red powder, which is the only reason he endured their insults for so many years.

There is no space here to enter into the entire question of the nature and objective reality of spirits, nor is it likely that any conclusions could be reached on this difficult subject.

Whatever is their essential nature, the Enochian angels acted as independent, intelligent beings with their own distinct personalities and purposes. This is how Dee and Kelly regarded them, and this is how I shall regard them in this essay, because I am presenting here the secret agenda of the angels, which they concealed from John Dee-to plant among mankind the ritual working that would initiate the period of violent transformation between the present Aeon and the next, commonly known as the Apocalypse.

THE GATES AND KEYS

What the Enochian angels conveyed to Dee through Kelly was not merely a more potent form of spirit magic to rule the tutelary daemons of the nations of the earth. It was an initiatory formula designed to open the locked gates of the four great Watchtowers that stand guard against chaos at the extremities of our universe. The Watchtowers are described by the angel Ave:

"The four houses', are the 4 Angels of the Earth, which are the 4 Overseers, and Watch-towers, that the eternal God in His providence hath placed, against usurping blasphemy, misuse, and stealth of the wicked and great enemy, the Devil. To the intent that being put out to the Earth, his envious will might be bridled, the determinations of God fulfilled, and his creatures kept and preserved, within the compass and measure of order."

These Watchtowers, represented in Enochian magic by alphabetical squares, are equivalent to the four mystical pillars of Egyptian mythology that hold up the sky and keep it from crashing into the earth. They bar the chaotic legions of Choronzon, the Enochian angels revealed to Dee, is the true heavenly name of **Satan**. He is also known by the Enochian title of Death-Dragon or Him-That-is-Fallen (Telocvovim).

The Enochian Calls, or Keys, the angels refer to them by both titles, are 48 spirit evocations delivered to Dee and Kelly in the Enochian language and then translated into English word for word by the angels. The overt purpose of the Keys, declared by the angels, is to enable Dee to establish ritual communication with the spirits of the 30 Aethers or Airs who rule over the tutelary daemons of the nations of the earth. There are actually 49 Keys, but the first, the angels informed Dee, is too sacred and mysterious to be voiced. The first eighteen explicit Keys are completely different in their wording; their last 30 are similar save for name of the Aether inserted in the first line.

The angel **Raphael** declares the expressed purpose of the keys to Dee:

"In 49 voyces or callings: which are the Natural Keys, to open those, not 49, but 48. For one is not to be opened. Gates of understanding, whereby you shall have knowledge to move every Gate, and to call out as many as you please, or shall be thought necessary, which can very well, righteously, and wisely, open unto you the secrets of their Cities & make you understand perfectly the contained in the tables."

The tables referred to by **Raphael** are the 49 alphabetical tables from which the Keys were generated, one letter at a time, by the Enochian angels. The Keys are related in sets to the Watchtowers, which contain the names of various hierarchies of spirits.

Dee's blindness to the true function of the Keys is curious, because clues about their nature are everywhere for those with eyes to see them. The Enochian communications recorded by Dee are filled with Apocalyptic pronouncements and imagery. Again and again the angels warn of the coming destruction of the world by the wrath of God and the advent of the Antichrist. This Apocalyptic imagery is also found throughout the Keys themselves.

The very name of these evocations should have been clue enough. Surely if the Watchtowers stand guard at the four corners of our dimension of reality, keeping back the hordes of Choronzon from descending like "stooping dragons," as the eighth Key puts it, and if the evocations known as the Keys are designed to open the gates of these Watchtowers, we might be led to suspect that it would be a bad idea to unlock the gates.

Perhaps Dee believed, as the angels deceitfully encouraged him to believe, that the gates could be opened a crack for a specific human purposes and then slammed shut before anything to horrible slipped through to our dimension of awareness. He would have assumed that the harrowing of the goddess Earth and her children by the daemons of Choronzon would occur until the preordained time of the Apocalypse, an event initiated by God and presumably beyond Dee's control.

What he failed to understand is that the date of the initiation of the period of change known as the Apocalypse is, in the intent of the angels, the same date as the successful completion of the full ritual working of the eighteen distinct manifest Keys and the Key of the thirty Aethers upon the Great Table of the Watchtowers, and that this date is not predetermined, but will be determined by the free will and actions of a single human being who is in the Revelation of St. John called the Antichrist.

THE NATURE OF THE APOCALYPSE

It has always been generally assumed that the Apocalypse is in the hands of the angels of wrath, to be visited upon the world at the pleasure of God, at a moment fore destined from the beginning of creation. In the veiled teachings of the Enochian angels this is not true. The Gates of the Watchtowers can only be unlocked from the inside. The angels of wrath cannot initiate the Apocalypse even if they wished today to do so. This is suggested by an exchange between Dee and the angel Ave:

Dee: As for the form of our Petition or invitation of the good Angels, what sort should it be of?
Ave: A short and brief speech.
Dee: We beseech you to give us an example: we would have a confidence it should be of more effect.
Ave: I may not do so.
Ave: Invocation proceeds of the good will of man, and of the heat and fervency of the spirit: And therefore is prayer of such effect with God.
Dee: We beseech you shall we use one form to all?
Ave: Every one, after a diverse form.
Dee: If the mind de dictate or prompt a diverse form, you mean.
Ave: I know not: for I dwell not in the soul of man.

Spiritual beings must be evoked into our reality by human beings. We must open the gates to admit the servants of Choronzon ourselves. Evocation and invocation are not a part of the business of angels, but of humans. That is why it was necessary for the Enochian angels to go through the elaborate ruse of conveying the system of Enochian magic, with the Keys and the Great Table of the Watchtowers, to Dee. If the Apocalypse is to take place, and if it is necessary for human beings to open the gates of the Watchtowers before it can take place, the angels first had to instruct a man in the correct method for opening the gates.

It is evident that Dee was to be restrained from opening the gates of the Watchtowers until it pleased the angels. The angel **Gabriel**, who purports to be speaking with the authority of God, Tells him:

"I have chosen you, to enter into my barns: And have commanded you to open the Corn that the scattered may appear, and that which remaineth in the sheaf may stand. And have entered into the first, and so into the seventh. And have delivered unto you a Testimony of my spirit to come.

"For my barn hath been long without threshers. And I have kept my flails for a long time hid in unknown places: Which flail is the Doctrine that I deliver unto you: Which instrument of thrashing, wherewith you shall beat the sheaves, that the Corn which is scattered and the rest may be all one.

"If I be Master of the Barn, owner of the Corn, and deliverer of my flail: If all be mine, and unto you, there is nothing: for you are hirelings, whose reward is in heaven. Then see that you neither thresh, nor unbind, until I bid you, let it be sufficient unto you: that you know my house, that you know the labor I will put you to: That I favor you so much as to entertain you the laborers within my barn: For within it threshes none without my consent."

Surely nothing could be ever clearer. Throughout the Enochian communications the angels refer to the Apocalypse euphemistically as "the Harvest." Here, Enochian magic is specifically described as the "instrument of thrashing." Yet Dee did not comprehend the awesome significance of the burden that had been laid upon his shoulders. Elsewhere in the record the angel Mapsama is just as explicit about the need for Dee to await permission before attempting to use the Keys:

Mapsama: These calls are the Keys into the Gates and Cities of wisdom, which are not able to be opened, but with visible apparition.

Dee: And how shall that be come unto?

Mapsama: Which is according to the former instructions: and to had, by calling of every table. You called for wisdom God hath opened unto you, His judgment: He hath delivered unto you the Keys, that you may enter; But be humble. Enter not of presumption, but of permission. Go not in rashly; But be brought in willingly: For, many have ascended, but few have entered. By Sunday you shall have all the things necessary to be taught; then, as occasion serves, you may practice at all times. But you are being called by God, and to a good purpose.

Dee: How shall we understand this calling by God?
Mapsama: God stops my mouth I will answer thee no more.

Despite these hints and many others, the angels never actually came out and told Dee that he was to be the instrument whereby the ritual formula that would initiate the Apocalypse would be planted in the midst of humanity, where it would sit like a ticking time bomb, waiting for some clever magician, perhaps guided by the angels, to work it. Dee evidently never received the signal to conduct the Apocalypse working in his lifetime. It was reserved for another century, and another man. That man was Aleister Crowley 1875-1947.

ENTER THE GREAT BEAST

Even as a child, Crowley became convinced that he was the Great Beast mentioned in the Biblical Book of Revelation. He studied magic within the Hermetic Order of the Golden Dawn, then went on to construct his own occult system using an amalgamation of the ritual working of Abramelin the Mage, the Goetia, and the Tantric sexual techniques of the German Ordo Templi Orientis among other sources.

He firmly believed that he was herald for a new age of strife and destruction that would sweep across the world. He called this the Aeon of Horus, after the Egyptian god of war. In 1909 in Cairo, Egypt, he received in the form of a psychic dictation from his guardian angel, Aiwass, the bible of this apocalyptic period, Liber AL vel Legis. The Book of the Law. It sets forth some of the conditions that will prevail in the Aeon of Horus. In it is Crowley's famous dictum: "Do what thou wilt shall be the whole of the Law."

It is highly significant that Crowley never considered himself to be the Antichrist. He is not the central character in the drama of the Apocalypse, but the herald who ushers in the age of chaos. In a very real sense he was the gatekeeper of the apocalypse. The text of the Book of the Law clearly states:

"This Book shall be translated into all tongues: but always with the original in the writing of the beast; for in the chance shape of the letters and their position to one another: in these are mysteries that no beast shall divine. Let him not seek to try: but one cometh after him, whence I say not, who shall discover the Key of it all."

Crowley studied and practiced Enochian magic more often and deeply than any other magician of the Golden Dawn; Indeed, more deeply than any other human being who has ever lived. About the angelic communications of Dee and Kelly he writes: Much of their work still defies explanation, though I and my initiates have spent much time and research upon it and cleared up many obscure points.

The record of his working of the Enochian Aethers in 1909 in the desert of North Africa is preserved in the document titled The Vision and the Voice. He possessed a profound and broad understanding of ritual magic, an understanding not merely theoretical but practical. No other man of the 20th century was better suited to initiate the Apocalypse Working, even as there had been no man better suited than John Dee in then16th century to receive it from the Enochian Angels. It is significant that Crowley believed himself the reincarnation of Edward Kelly.

I doubt that Crowley ever succeeded in correctly completing the entire Enochian Apocalypse Working -that is primal occult Key which is nowhere recorded, the eighteen manifest Keys and the Key of the Thirty Aethers in their correct correspondence with parts of the Great Table of the Watchtowers-but he may have succeeded in partially opening the Gates of the Watchtowers. It is significant that he states concerning the African working with his disciple: "As a rule, we did one Aethyr every day." About the method of working the Keys the angel Ave tells Dee:

"Four days must you only call upon those names of God, on the Great Table of the Watchtowers, or on the God of Hosts, in those names:

"And 14 days after you shall, in this, or in some convenient place, Call the Angels by petition and by the name of God, unto the which they are obedient. The 15 day you shall Cloth yourselves, in vestures made of linen: white: and so have the apparition, use and practice of the Creatures. For, it is not a labor of years, not many days."

It seems clear to me that the complete Apocalypse Working, which will be conducted by the Antichrist and will throw wide the gates of the Watchtowers, If we are to believe the intimations of the Enochian angels must be conducted on consecutive days, one Key per day. I would guess that the unexpressed primordial Key of the Great Mother is the missing ingredient that will complete the Working, but this is a matter of practical magic and there is no space to investigate the details of the Apocalypse Working in this brief essay.

Crowley remained firmly convinced until his death in 1947 that the Aeon of Horus had begun in 1904, precisely at the time he received The Book of the Law. He may have been right. The Aeon of Horus is the duration of the Apocalpyse, that period when Choronzon shall rule over the cosmos and visit destruction upon mankind. And the Apocalypse is a mental transformation that will occur, or is presently occurring, within the collective conscious of the human race.

A MENTAL ARMAGEDDON

It is common among fundamentalist Christians to believe that the end of the world will be a completely physical event and will be sparked by some horrifying material agent-global thermonuclear war, or the impact of a large asteroid, or a deadly plague.

This supposition is natural in view of the concrete imagery in the vision of St John the Divine, the purported author of Revelations. It is in keeping with the materialistic world view of modern society. But nobody stops to consider that this destruction is described by angels, or that angels are spiritual creatures, not physical beings.

In my opinion the Apocalypse prepared by the Enochian angels must be primarily in internal, spiritual event, and only in a secondary way an external physical catastrophe. The gates of the Watchtowers that stand guard at the four corners of our dimension of reality are mental constructions. When they are opened, they will admit the demons of Choronzon, not into the physical world, but into our subconscious minds.

Spirits are mental, not material. They dwell in the depths of mind and communicate with us through our dreams, unconscious impulses, and more rarely in waking visions. They affect our feelings and our thoughts beneath the level of our conscious awareness. Sometimes they are able to control our actions, either partially as in the case of irrational and obsessive behavior patterns, or completely as in the case of full possession. Through us, by using us as their physical instruments, and only through us, are they able to influence physical things.

The Enochian communications teach us that not only must humanity itself initiate the cosmic drama of the Apocalypse through the magical formula delivered to John Dee and Edward Kelly more than four centuries ago, but humans must also be the physical actors that bring about the plagues, wars and famines, described with such chilling eloquence in the vision of St. John. We must let in the demons of Choronzon into our minds by means of a specific ritual working. They will not find a welcome place there all at once, but will worm their way into our subconscious and make their homes there slowly over time. In the minds of individuals that resist this invasion they will find it difficult to gain a foothold, but in the more pliable minds of those who welcome their influence they will establish themselves readily.

Once they have taken up residence, we will be powerless to prevent them turning our thoughts and actions toward chaotic and destructive ends. These Apocalypse spirits will set person against person and nation against nation, gradually increasing the degree of madness, or chaos, in human society, until at last the full horror of Revelation has been realized upon the stage of the world. The corruption of human thoughts and feelings may require generations to bring to full fruition. Only after the wasting and burning of souls is well advanced will the full horror of the Apocalypse achieve its fulfillment in the material realm.

Let us suppose for the sake of argument that the signal for the initiation of this psychic invasion occurred in 1904 when Crowley received The Book of the Law, as Crowley himself believed. Crowley's Enochian evocations of 1909 then pried the doors of the Watchtowers open a crack-enough to allow a foul wind through the common subconscious mind of the human race. This would explain the senseless slaughter of the First World War and the unspeakable horror of the Nazi Holocaust during the Second World War. It would explain the decline of organized religions and why the soulless cult of science has gained supremacy. It would explain the moral and ethical bankruptcy of modern times and the increase in senseless crimes of violence.

We may not have long to wait before the individual known in the vision of St. John as the Antichrist, the one foretold in Crowley's The Book of the Law to follow after the Beast, will succeed in completing the Apocalypse Working placed in the world as a flaming sword by the Enochian angels. Then the gates of the Watchtowers will truly gape wide, and the children of Choronzon will sweep into our minds as crowned conquerors, if this chilling mythic scenario ever comes to pass, the wars of the 20th century will seem bucolic to those who survive the slaughter.

About the Author

Dear Reader,

    My name is Ernest Johnson. If this letter reaches your eyes and ears, then pay attention to the details. Our galaxy is fully occupied by the unseen gods. All of them are positioning themselves to bring about the Judgment of End Times. All heavenly forces and wicked forces have their agenda. They are all active. They all have hardened positions and winner takes all. Where we are at on the great apocalypse time clock is alarming to say the least. I speak to all conscious beings, both dead and alive, to support anyone, anywhere who can bring you deep knowledge that will enlighten our understanding on the unforeseen forces.

    Deeply you know this subject I'm speaking of. You instinctively understand what is at stake. You know you heart beats to your dream. To be faceless is to be enlightened. Give up self to allow the energy of these forces to lead you to your destiny, whatever it is, for only you decide.

I have been from heaven to hell to bring to you the nasty facts of life. BS/No BS razor's edge, set on fire by the Holy Spirit. I can only be your friend by not becoming your friend. My material is not the light hearted. You may not be suited for my writings.

Duality is misleading if we judge from this place. Church is not what it seems. Hell is neither Christ or Satan! Truth is, your reality is only that, your own reality. I have brought to you Earth shattering, thunder thinking. You will learn by subjecting yourself to this new cutting edge, bone shattering thunder. Only then can you appreciate the spirit of man.

If you think this letter is either honest or deceptive, you are right either way. But do us both a favor, reread this letter. Act with love or hatred. Either one will work. Just educate yourself in any way you choose. But learn, you must do. We live in a world that doesn't understand deep inner things. But we all crave it. My material is my best that this hard-working man of iron can muster. Honesty and truth are not the same. The church is not what is seems. My material is designed to clear all the cobwebs, address the sin of man from a dual mind set, with quadruple points of view.

This is why nothing is as it seems. Learn why you're here. What your mission is. What your part is. Last but not least, where you'll end up.

This is how I present my audio. It's shut up, sit your ass down and listen to what the gods have to say to you. Period! But not all at once. Each subject is just that, one subject. But all combined, Yes! After continuing for a season you will understand this to be true!

Stand for something or fall for anything! The cosmic gates are about to swing wide. Support for this cause is paramount. Capture the energy, capture the matter. Live life on the run!

Whatever it is that you desire, first rule is to lock yourself into the energy of it. Look deeply into the subject and dive in.

That's it. Secret revealed! All success is wrapped up in this key!
Ernest Johnson

www.ingramcontent.com/pod-product-compliance
Lightning Source LLC
LaVergne TN
LVHW041625070426
835507LV00008B/450